Workbook

MORE! 2

Gerngross · Puchta
Holzmann · Lewis-Jones · Stranks

HELBLING

Liebe Schülerin, lieber Schüler!

Neben vielen Übungen, mithilfe derer du deine Kenntnisse der englischen Sprache erweitern und festigen kannst, findest du im Workbook am Ende jeder Unit auch eine Auflistung des Lernvokabulars, also der wichtigsten Wörter und Phrasen aus der jeweiligen Unit.

Diese Wortlisten sind in zwei Abschnitte unterteilt:

1. Word File

Unter dieser Überschrift werden jene Wörter und Ausdrücke nochmals aufgelistet / dargestellt, die im Student's Book eingeführt werden.

2. MORE Words and Phrases

In diesem Abschnitt findest du die wichtigsten Wörter aus der jeweiligen Unit im Student's Book. Sie sind in der Reihenfolge aufgelistet, wie sie im Student's Book vorkommen, und zur leichteren Orientierung auch mit der jeweiligen Nummer einer Aktivität aus dem Student's Book gekennzeichnet: ❶, ❷ usw.

Wichtig: Jene Wörter und Wortgruppen, die fett gedruckt sind, werden im Englischen sehr häufig verwendet. Du solltest sie gut beherrschen.

Zusatzinformation: Der Vollständigkeit halber soll auch noch darauf hingewiesen werden, dass es natürlich viele andere Wörter gibt, die im Student's Book eingeführt werden, die aber im Lernvokabular im Workbook nicht vorkommen. Der Grund dafür ist, dass sie im Alltag nicht so häufig gebraucht werden und daher nicht zum eigentlichen Lernvokabular gehören. Du findest sie alle – alphabetisch gereiht – in der Nachschlagliste am Ende deines Student's Book. Mithilfe dieser Liste kannst du schnell die Bedeutung neu vorgekommener Wörter nachschlagen.

Noch ein Tipp: Wer eine Sprache gut beherrschen möchte, sollte darauf achten, dass sein Wortschatz ständig wächst. Das heißt aber auch, dass man schon gelernte Wörter und Phrasen regelmäßig wiederholen muss. Geh deshalb immer wieder die Liste mit den Wörtern und Phrasen der vorangegangenen Units durch – du solltest dir davon möglichst alle gut merken!

Answer key

Wenn du deine Ergebnisse überprüfen möchtest, findest du am Ende des Buches alle Lösungen für die Übungen im Workbook.

MORE! WORKBOOK 2
by Günter Gerngross, Herbert Puchta, Christian Holzmann, Peter Lewis-Jones, Jeff Stranks

Edited by Johanna Schmölzer, Christina Freudenschuss-Heigl

Design and layout by Heinz Hanuschka, Amanda Hockin

Illustrated by Roberto Battestini, Francesca Carabelli, Sergio Cingolani, Giovanni Giorgi Pierfranceschi, Svjetlan Junaković, Roberta Maddalena, Mirella Mariani, Björn Pertoft, Giovanni Rolandi, Lorenzo Sabbatini, Matteo Settegrana

Printed by Athesia

First published 2017, third print run 2019

Workbook:
ISBN 978-3-99045-056-7

Workbook + E-BOOK+:
ISBN 978-3-99089-015-8

SBNR 135.561 (Workbook)
SBNR 190.456 (Workbook + E-BOOK+)

www.helblinglanguages.at

Contents

Zeichenerklärung

1	Diese Übung enthält wichtige Inhalte und sollte nicht ausgelassen werden.
2	Diese Übung kann bei Zeitmangel im Sinne eines "Fast track" durch die Unit ohne Probleme ausgelassen werden.
3 CHOICES	Bei dieser Übung stehen dir zwei Varianten zur Verfügung.
G	Grammar
SB p. 15	Diese Übung passt zur angegebenen Seite im Student's Book (Seite 15).
SWYK Units 1–4	Hier gibt es im Internet (www.helbling-ezone.com) die Möglichkeit, deinen Lernfortschritt einzuschätzen (*Show what you know*).

UNIT 1 Welcome back

Essential Vocabulary

1 Write the words under the pictures.

French
Geography
Maths
History
Design and Technology
Music
Physical Education
Science
Art
English
Information Technology

1 ....

2 ....

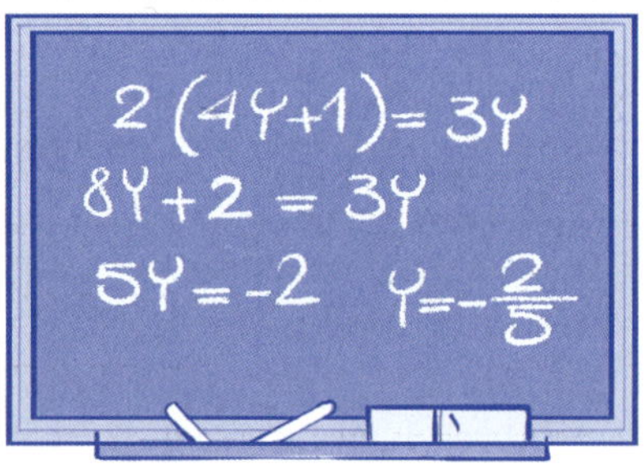

3 ....

4 ....

5 ....

6 ....

7 ....

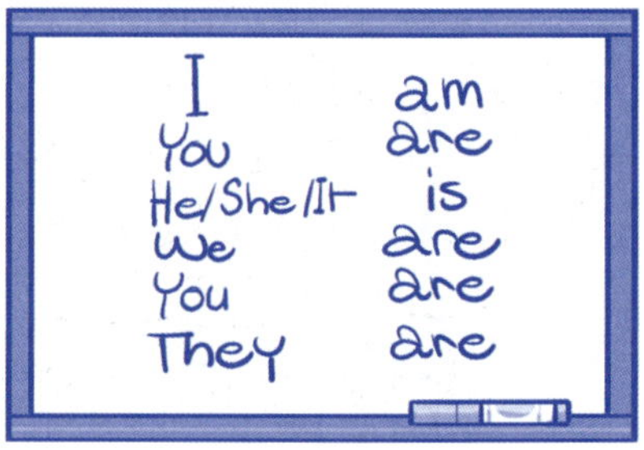

8 ....

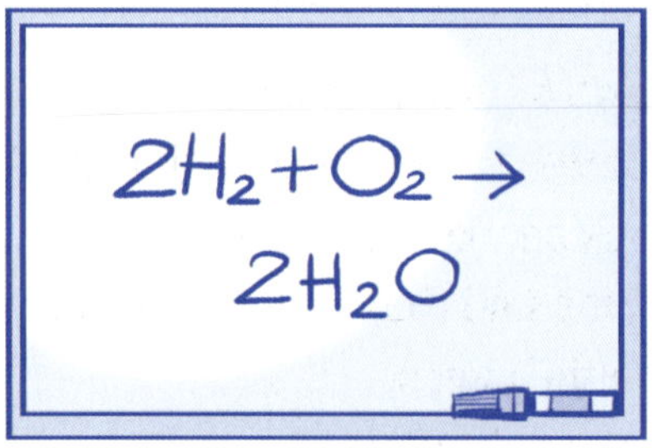

9 ....

10 ....

11 ....

SB p. 10

More Vocabulary

2 Complete the timetable.

	Monday	Tuesday	Wednesday	Thursday	Friday
9–9.55 a.m.	....	....	....	....	....
10–10.55	....	....	....	....	....
Break					
11.15 a.m. – 12.10 p.m.	....	....	....	....	....
Lunch					
1–1.55 p.m.	....	....	....	....	....
2–2.35		....	....	....	....
2.40–3.15	....	....		....	

3 Who has got what on Monday at 1 o'clock? Write sentences.

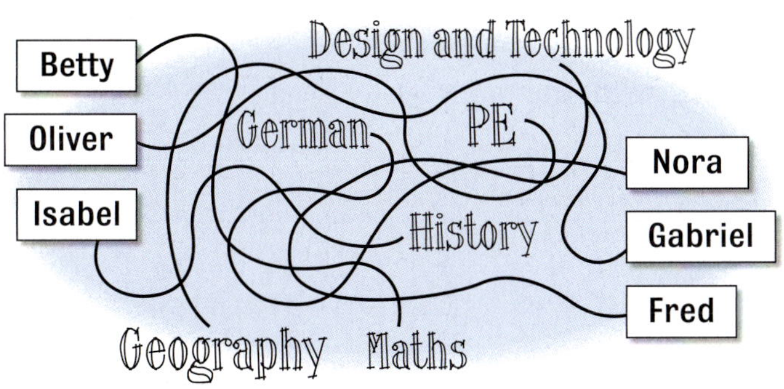

1 Betty has got Maths on Monday at 1 o'clock.
2 ....
3 ....
4 ....
5 ....
6 ....

Reading and Writing

4 Match the sentence halves for a summary of the story *First day at school.*

1 On the first day of the new school
2 Sara's story was the first
3 Sara and her family went
4 They had a great time swimming and
5 One day, Sara's brother came
6 There was a strange blue and
7 Sara remembered about the blue-ringed
8 She saved her brother's life because

☐ octopus and hit her brother's hand.
☐ back from the sea with a beautiful shell.
☐ the octopus can kill you with one bite.
☐ year the kids told their holiday stories.
☐ playing on the beach.
☐ and also the only story.
☐ to Australia.
☐ yellow thing inside and he wanted to pull it out.

SB p. 10, 11

5 **Read the texts. How many of the tasks below can you do?**

Fatih (Turkey): Hi, my name's Fatih. I'm twelve and I've got two sisters and two brothers. I live in a village about 50 kilometres from Istanbul. My favourite food is Lahmacun. It's like pizza. I like video games and nature programmes. I also play football and I swim a lot. With my pocket money (it's not much) I buy sweets. I don't have a pet, because my mum doesn't like animals.

Clare (Scotland): Hi, I'm Clare. I live in Dundee in Scotland. I'm twelve. I've got one brother. He's 21 and he works in Edinburgh. My favourite food is chicken. And I also like chocolate a lot. My friend Moira and I often go to the park (we're skateboarders) and in the evenings we watch TV together. We like sitcoms best. I also like reading (Moira doesn't, she doesn't want to read the Harry Potter books) and horse riding. I've got two pets – a cat and a guinea pig.

Justyna (Poland): Hi, I'm Justyna. I live in Krakow and I've got two little brothers. I'm thirteen and my brothers are five and eight. My favourite food is fish, but we don't eat it very often. I play handball in our school team and I'm also in the swimming team. I love going to the cinema. A lot of films are in English. That's good for me. I can listen to English a lot. I buy magazines with my pocket money. I haven't got a pet.

Sean (Ireland): Hi, I'm Sean, I'm from Sligo in Ireland. I live on a farm and I really like animals. We've got lots of animals, but I don't have a real pet. We've got six horses and I really like horse riding. My friends and I also play football and computer games. I often help at home. My dad gives me some pocket money for that. I buy computer games with the money. My favourite food is pizza.

Circle T (*True*) or F (*False*).

1 Fatih has got four sisters. T / F

2 Lahmacun is a type of food. T / F

3 Fatih gets a lot of pocket money. T / F

Complete the sentences.

4 Clare is .... younger than her brother.

5 Clare and Moira like .... in the daytime.

6 Justyna is in the school team for ....

Answer the questions.

7 What are Justyna's hobbies? ....

8 Why does Sean's family have room for six horses? ....

9 What does Sean spend his money on? ....

6 **Check your answers.**

SB p. 9

Essential Grammar Present simple (revision)

7 Write short answers.

1 Does Jane play tennis on Tuesday afternoons? (✓) Yes, she does.
2 Does she go to bed early on Friday evenings? (✗) ....
3 Does she often go shopping with her mum at the weekend? (✓) ....
4 Does she go to school on Sundays? (✗) ....
5 Does she go skating on Saturday afternoons? (✗) ....
6 Does she watch TV every evening? (✓) ....
7 Does she like pizza and chips? (✗) ....
8 Does she phone her best friend every day? (✓) ....

Essential Grammar Past simple (revision)

8 Match the pictures with the sentences.

1 In the morning I watched TV.
2 At lunchtime I played computer games.
3 In the afternoon I played beach volleyball.
4 In the evening I went to the cinema.
5 And after the cinema I read a book.
6 After my holidays I was really tired.

A

B

C

D

E

F

9 Find eight more past forms (← → ↑ ↓ ↗).

fell

....

....

....

....

....

....

....

....

U	W	Z	D	K	T
M	C	R	A	N	O
S	A	F	E	L	L
A	M	W	R	H	D
W	E	R	E	N	O
U	A	A	D	A	H

SB p. 13

More Grammar Present simple (revision)

10 Complete the questions.

Interviewer 1 Where does the blue-ringed octopus live ?
Expert It lives in warm water.
Interviewer 2 How many .... ?
Expert It has got eight arms.
Interviewer 3 What .... ?
Expert It's dark yellow, but it can turn bright yellow. And it has blue rings, of course.
Interviewer 4 What .... ?
Expert It eats fish.
Interviewer 5 Is .... ?
Expert Yes, the poison is very strong. It can kill a man.
Interviewer 6 Is .... ?
Expert No, there's no medicine against the poison. So it's very dangerous.

11 Complete the sentences with your own ideas.

1 I never play computer games after school. .... (never / play)
2 My best friend .... (always / phone)
3 My mum .... (usually / go)
4 I .... (sometimes / watch)
5 I .... (often / listen)
6 My dad .... (never / do)

More Grammar Past simple (revision)

12 Find the verbs in the word snake and write them in the past simple.

sitholdremembermeetgolovereadtakerunput

1 sit – sat
2 .... – ....
3 .... – ....
4 .... – ....
5 .... – ....
6 .... – ....
7 .... – ....
8 .... – ....
9 .... – ....
10 .... – ....

13 Use some of the verbs in 12 to complete the sentences.

1 When I was young, I .... my mum's hand all the way to school.
2 I .... my little sister to the cinema last night.
3 We were late so we .... for the school bus this morning.
4 I'm sure I .... my homework in my school bag last night. So where is it now?
5 The film was really long. We .... in the cinema for three hours!
6 Our family .... to Jamaica on holiday this year.
7 My sister .... the Queen last year.
8 I .... the TV show *Teletubbies* when I was a little kid.

SB p. 12, 13

14 Write the verbs in brackets* in the past simple.

The shell on the beach

I [1]...................... (see) a really nice shell on the beach. I [2]...................... (pick) it up because I [3]...................... (want) to show it to Mum. "Oh Michael," Mum [4]...................... (say), "that looks lovely. What a nice shell." "And it has got something blue and yellow inside. Do you want to see it?" I said. Suddenly my sister Sara [5]...................... (hit) my hand and [6]...................... (shout): "Don't touch it." "Ouch!" I [7]...................... (say). "What's wrong?"

"Sara!" Mum [8]...................... (say), "leave Michael alone." "But look!" Sara [9]...................... (shout), and [10]...................... (point) at the nice shell. "There's a blue-ringed octopus inside. It can kill you!" There, lying in the sand [11]...................... (be) a little octopus. It [12]...................... (look) nice, but Mum [13]...................... (say), "Don't touch it!" And she [14]...................... (hug) me and then she [15]...................... (hug) Sara.

VOCABULARY: *bracket – Klammer

15 Write sentences about Olivia's holiday last month.

1 Olivia went to a museum.
....
....

2 ....
....
....
....

3 ....
....
....
....

4 ....
....
....
....

5 ....
....
....
....

6 ....
....
....
....

7 ....
....
....
....

16 Use the notes to write a short text about what Kevin did last Saturday. Use some of your own ideas too.

Saturday
Morning: get up late / watch TV / lunch
Afternoon: football match with dad
Evening: dinner in restaurant / bed late

Last Saturday Kevin got up late.
He got up very late. He got up at 11 a.m.!
Then ...

SB p. 8, 11, 13

WORD FILE

My timetable

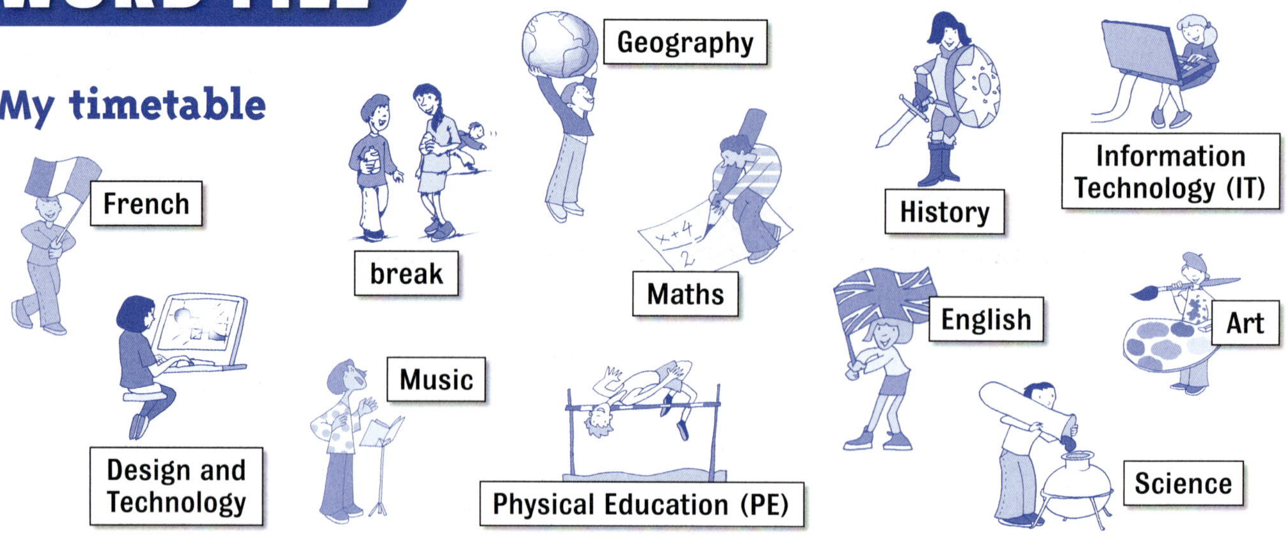

MORE Words and Phrases

2	**as soon as**	*As soon as I get up in the morning, I go to the bathroom.*	sobald
	finish	*I finish school at 4 o'clock.*	beenden
	get dressed	*I get dressed in the morning when I get up.*	sich anziehen
	go for a walk	*We often go for a walk in the park.*	spazieren gehen
	important	*It's very important to have good friends.*	wichtig
	last	*Our English lesson lasts for 40 minutes.*	dauern
	right away	*When school finishes, I go home right away.*	sofort
3	**daily**	*My daily routine starts when I get up in the morning.*	täglich
5	**timetable**	*She has four English lessons in her timetable.*	Stundenplan
6	bite	*This snake's bite is poisonous.*	Biss
	everyone	*Come here, everyone!*	jede/r; alle
	north	*My uncle lives in the north of England.*	nördlich, Nord-; Norden
	on one's own	*Joe wasn't married. He lived on his own.*	allein, auf sich gestellt
	octopus (pl -es)	*An octopus has eight arms.*	Krake
	poisonous	*The blue-ringed octopus is poisonous.*	giftig
	shell	*I like collecting shells on the beach.*	Muschel
	So what?	*"Sue has got a pony." "So what? My sister has got a horse."*	Na und?
	somewhere	*They always go somewhere exciting.*	irgendwo
9	**against**	*There is no medicine against the poison.*	gegen
	attacker	*The insect uses poison to kill its attacker.*	Angreifer/in
	bright	*I love bright colours.*	hell, leuchtend
	dangerous	*The blue-ringed octopus is very dangerous.*	gefährlich
	hunt	*Some animals hunt at night.*	jagen
	medicine (no pl)	*Do you need medicine?*	Medizin; Medikament/e
	poison	*Poison can kill you.*	Gift
	size	*What size shoes do you take?*	Größe
	turn	*The octopus turns yellow when you attack it.*	werden
11	**back**	*I hurt my back when I fell over.*	Rücken
	cover	*Cover the computer before ink gets on that, too!*	bedecken
	furious	*She has got food all over her new jeans – she's furious.*	wütend
	hug	*We hugged each other and said goodbye.*	umarmen
	ink	*I can't write. I haven't got any ink in my pen.*	Tinte
	shake	*Did you shake the octopus' arm?*	schütteln
	sight	*This is quite a sight!*	Aussicht; Anblick
	tight	*My shoes are too tight.*	fest; eng

Did we catch them?

Essential Vocabulary

1 Look at the picture. Write the numbers next to the words.

- ☐ arrest
- ☐ break into
- ☐ footprints
- ☐ alarm
- ☐ police station
- ☐ blood
- 5 sergeant
- ☐ steal
- ☐ fingerprint
- ☐ guard
- ☐ police
- ☐ go off
- ☐ thief

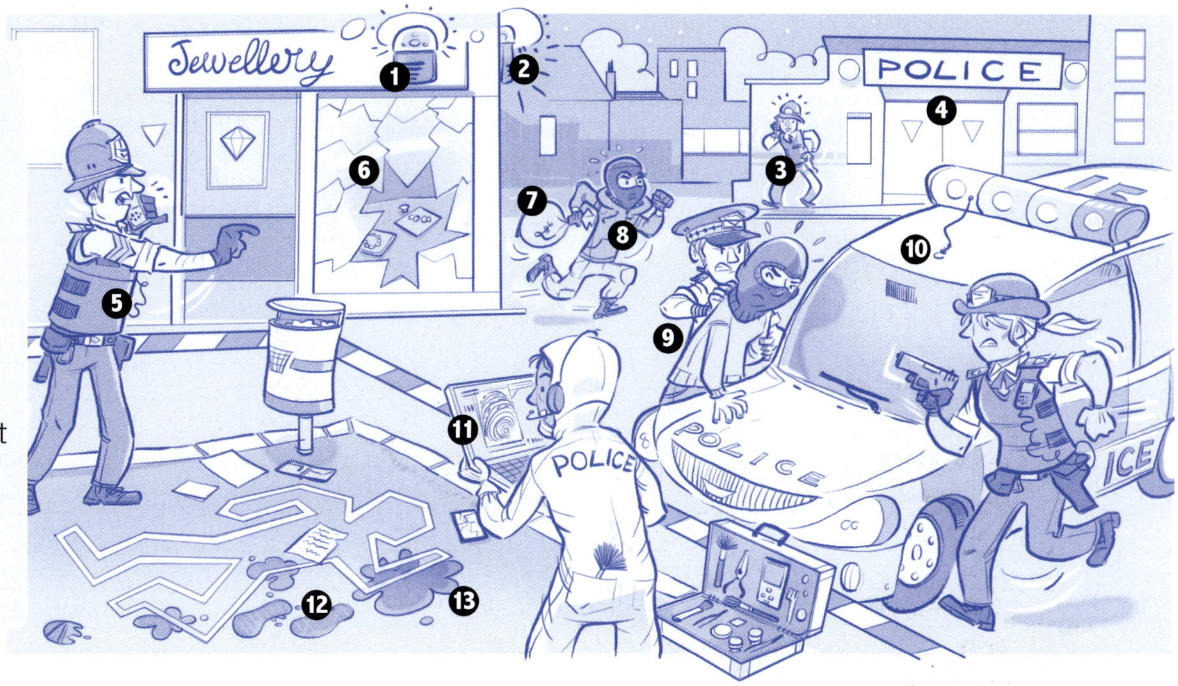

2 Read and complete. Use words from 1. Sometimes you need to change the form.

A There are two police [1]s............................ in front of the museum.

B Yes, I know. A man [2]b............................ i............................ the museum last night and [3]st............................ a painting.

A Aren't there any [4]g............................ at night?

B No, there is no security at night, but the [5]a............................ [6]w............................ o............................ .

A So did the [7]p............................ [8]a............................ the [9]th............................ ?

B No, they didn't. But there were [10]fi............................ and [11]f............................ . And they found some [12]b............................ on the floor. I'm sure they'll find the thief soon!

More Vocabulary

3 Write the words.

1 A person who steals money from another person is a ....

2 When the alarm .... , a bell starts ringing.

3 When you touch glass, the police can find .... on it.

4 When you cut your finger, ... will come out.

5 If you want to talk to a police sergeant, go to the ....

6 A .... is a person who cares for the security of other people.

7 They lost the key, so they had to .... their own house!

8 When the police arrived and saw that the man had a gun, they .... him.

SB p. 14–18

4 Find the words and write them under the pictures. (↓ →)

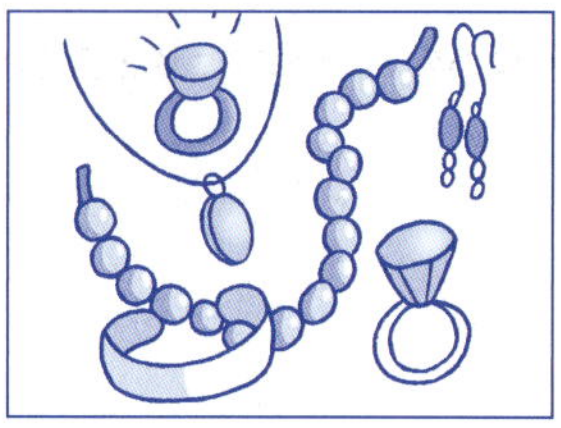

1 ....

2 ....

A	S	S	I	S	T	A	N	T
S	W	T	C	H	E	M	F	E
S	A	G	J	E	W	E	L	S
I	T	E	E	T	A	D	O	T
T	C	O	L	H	L	A	O	O
A	H	S	W	A	L	L	R	I
C	S	T	A	G	E	W	B	F
H	Y	P	N	O	T	I	S	T

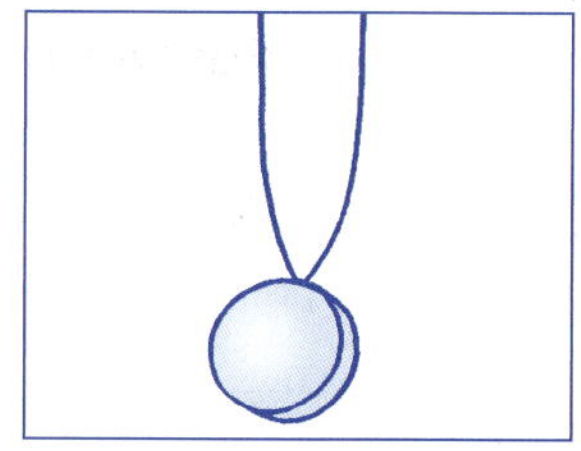

8 ....

7 ....

3 ....

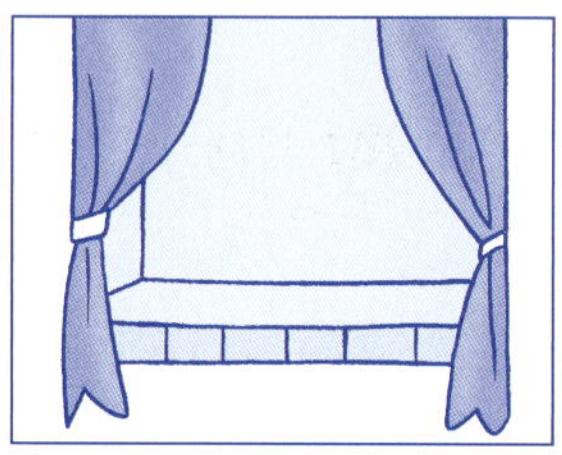

4 ....

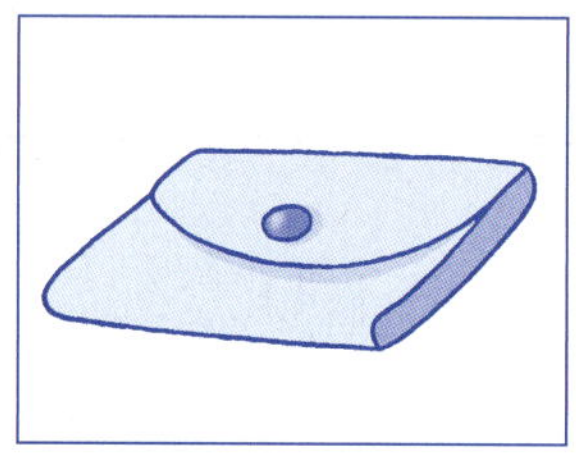

5 ....

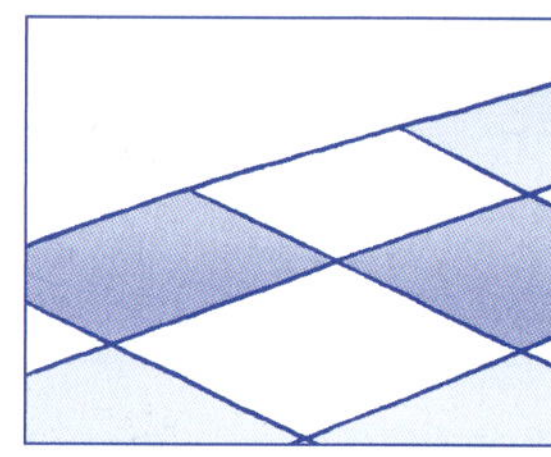

6 ....

Reading and Writing

5 Read about the play *Pronto!* Underline the six mistakes.

Roger and Claire went to a hypnotist show. The hypnotist, Charles, hypnotised Roger with a watch. The hypnotist took Roger's wallet from him. Roger woke up when the hypnotist said "Abracadabra".

But the man also gave Roger some secret commands. Roger broke into a shop and stole some jewels. Then he jumped out of the window.

But he left his wallet there, and the police found it. Inspector Lime went to Roger and Claire's house to investigate* the crime. But Roger wasn't there – he was in hospital.

Sergeant Lewis went to the hospital with Claire to talk to Roger, but he didn't react. Roger woke up when a doctor said the secret word. Claire told the police about the hypnotist.

The police caught the hypnotist and his friend in Hong Kong.

VOCABULARY: *investigate – untersuchen

6 Write sentences. Correct the mistakes in 5.

1 Charles hypnotised Roger with a medal.
2 ....
3 ....
4 ....
5 ....
6 ....

SB p. 14–18

7 CHOICES

A Put the sentences in the correct order and write the story in your exercise book.

- [ ] She phoned Inspector Lime. "There's a thief in my house," she said.
- [ ] When the thief ran away, Inspector Lime tripped him up* and arrested him.
- [ ] When Mrs Jones got home, she saw some lights in her house.
- [ ] Five minutes later the Inspector arrived. He had a great idea.

VOCABULARY: *trip somebody up – jemandem ein Bein stellen

B Look at the pictures. Write the story. Use the words in the box to help you.

The lost money

broke the vase	saw a vase
found the money	angry
fell over the cat	picked up
went to her house	gave
very happy	~~phoned~~

One day Mrs Jones phoned Inspector Lime. She said: "I can't find my money." Inspector Lime went ...

8 CHOICES

A Complete the dialogue with the words in the box.

find
found
~~took~~
take
have
use
put
jumped

A Did you hear about the robbery last week?

B No. What happened?

A Two men broke into a bank in the High Street. They [1]......took...... a lot of money and [2].............................. it into bags. Then they [3].............................. out of a window.

B Why didn't they [4].............................. the door?

A They didn't [5].............................. the key!

B Oh, right! Did the police find them?

A No – but they [6].............................. the money!

B Really? Where did they [7].............................. it?

A In the bank. The two men didn't [8].............................. the bags with them!!

B Put the dialogue in the correct order.

☐ **Lewis** Did they talk to you?
☐ **Lewis** Why did he hit him?
☐ **Lewis** Did you and your friends go to the bank?
☐ **Lewis** Did you see anyone in the bar?
1 **Lewis** Where were you at 8 o'clock last night?
☐ **Witness** No, we didn't. We went to a bar.
☐ **Witness** Yes, I did. I saw two men. They were at another table.
☐ **Witness** No, they didn't. But one man looked very angry and he hit the other man!
☐ **Witness** I was in the High Street. I went there with my friends.
☐ **Witness** I don't know – but he shouted "You fool! Why did you leave the bags in the bank?"

Essential Grammar Past simple negation (revision)

9 Rewrite the sentences. Make them negative.

1 I enjoyed the show.
I didn't enjoy the show.

2 Paul went to school today.
Paul didn't ....

3 The dogs chased the cat.
....

4 Lana took Owen's milk.
....

5 The children played computer games all morning.
....

SB p. 19

10 **Complete with the words in the box.**

~~went~~
didn't go
didn't have
found
didn't find
took
didn't take

Bill Gunn and Tony Bull stole money from the bank last night. They [1] ......went...... to the bank and broke a window. They [2] .... the money from the safe and put it in bags. Then they jumped out of a window. They [3] .... out through* the door because they [4] .... the key. But Bill [5] .... the bags with him! The police [6] .... the thieves, but they [7] .... the money.

VOCABULARY: *through – durch

Essential Grammar Past simple questions

11 **Match the questions and answers.**

1 Did you go to Jim's party?	☐	Yes, it did and I'm not very happy with it.
2 Did you go away for your holidays?	☐	Yes, it did. All day!
3 Did it rain yesterday?	☐	No, they didn't. Not a word.
4 Did Dave like his present?	☐	Yes, she did. Lots of it.
5 Did Lucy ride her bike to school?	☐	No, we didn't. We stayed at home.
6 Did they say anything?	☐	Yes, I did. I danced a lot.
7 Did the teacher give us homework?	☐	No, she didn't. Her dad took her in the car.
8 Did the dog break the vase?	☐	Yes, he did. He loved it.

12 **Complete with the short answers (*Yes, I did / No, I didn't*).**

1 Did you have a good holiday?
(✓) .... I went to New York.

2 Did you do a lot of shopping?
(✗) .... I visited lots of famous places.

3 Did you go to the Statue of Liberty?
(✓) .... I went to the top of it.

4 Did you go to Central Park?
(✓) .... I had a picnic there.

5 Did you send me a postcard?
(✗) .... Sorry. I didn't have time.

More Grammar Past simple negation (revision)

13 **Complete the sentences using the verbs in brackets in the past.**

1 Sue .... on holiday, but she .... me a postcard. (go / not send)
2 We .... the film because we .... late at the cinema. (not see / arrive)
3 Billy .... anything because he .... hungry. (not eat / not be)
4 I .... you because I .... your number. (not phone / lose)
5 I .... the film, but I .... the book. (see / not read)
6 Jessie .... me to her party, but I .... (invite / not go)
7 We .... anything because there .... nothing in the fridge. (not cook / be)
8 The band .... until midnight, but we .... to the end. (play / not stay)

SB p. 19, 20

14 Write the verbs in brackets in the past simple.

Hi Simone,

I [1] ..didn't phone.. (not phone) you, because the phone [2] .... (not work). And I [3] .... (not send) you an email, because the computer [4] .... (not work). And I [5] .... (not buy) you a present, because I [6] .... (not have) any money. And I [7] .... (not get) you any chocolate, because I [8] .... (not know) which chocolate you like. So I [9] .... (not go) to your party and I [10] .... (not make) a birthday cake for you. But happy birthday anyway!

More Grammar Past simple questions

15 Complete the questions and the short answers.

1 A ..Did.. they ..arrive.. after midnight? (arrive)
B Yes, ..they did.. .

2 A .... you .... your trip? (enjoy)
B No, ...

3 A .... your parents .... with you? (go)
B No, ...

4 A .... you .... a lot? (swim)
B Yes, ...

5 A .... you .... by bus? (go)
B Yes, ...

6 A .... she .... you a postcard? (write)
B No, ...

7 A .... they .... the hotel? (like)
B No, ...

8 A .... your mum .... a lot? (talk)
B No, she ....

16 Answer the questions so they are true for you.

1 Did you go to school yesterday?
....

2 Did you phone any friends yesterday?
....

3 Did your best friend phone you yesterday?
....

4 Did you watch TV last night?
....

5 Did you go to the cinema last weekend?
....

6 Did your class have a test last week?
....

SB p. 20

WORD FILE

Police

MORE Words and Phrases

1	assistant	*His assistant helps him on stage.*	Assistent/in
	wallet	*I have my money in my wallet.*	Brieftasche
2	alarm	*When he broke into the house, the alarm went off.*	Alarm
	already	*They were already on the train to London.*	bereits, schon
	applause	*The applause at the end of the play was very loud.*	Beifall
	background	*In the background you can see the broken window.*	Hintergrund
	both	*They both laugh.*	beide
	character	*What character are you in the play?*	Charakter; hier: Person
	clean	*My shoes are clean.*	sauber
	command	*The boss gives commands.*	Befehl
	dirty	*I must clean my dirty shoes.*	dreckig, schmutzig
	do the washing-up	*Do the washing-up – and do it pronto!*	abwaschen
	doctor	*I'm ill! I need a doctor.*	Arzt, Ärztin
	fact	*Tell me the facts.*	Fakten, Tatsachen
	gentleman	*Ladies and gentlemen! Welcome!*	Herr
	girlfriend	*Roger's new girlfriend is very clever.*	feste Freundin
	hop	*She hops around on one leg.*	hüpfen
	I don't care.		Das ist mir egal.
	jewel	*All her jewels are in a drawer in her bedroom.*	Juwel
	kiss	*My mum kissed me and said goodnight.*	küssen
	mess	*The room is in a terrible mess.*	Durcheinander, Chaos
	office	*Inspector Lime's office is at the police station.*	Büro
	have a seat	*Please, have a seat Inspector Lime.*	Platz nehmen
	secret	*Vivien gave Roger the secret commands.*	geheim
	security guard	*John works as a security guard at a big factory.*	Wächter/in
	shock	*After the accident the man is in shock.*	Schock(zustand)
	stiff	*My neck's stiff. I can't move my head.*	steif
	still	*It was late, but the streets were still full of people.*	noch, noch immer
	swing	*The hypnotist was swinging a watch in front of me.*	(hin- und her-)schwingen
3	by accident	*I gave her the wrong book by accident.*	versehentlich
5	**the dishes**	*I always help with the dishes after dinner.*	Geschirr(spülen)
	go for a run	*Let's go for a run in the park.*	laufen gehen
7	**expensive**	*This watch was very expensive.*	teuer
	large	*I saw a man with a large bag.*	groß
	witness	*After the accident the police spoke to a witness.*	Zeuge, Zeugin

More Grammar *why – because*

11 **Look at the pictures and write sentences with *because*. Use the words in the box.**

phone him
go to the dentist's*
have toothache*
see a face at the window
have a cold*
stay in bed
~~be happy~~
be scared

1 He was happy because Janice phoned him.

2 ....

3 ....

4 ....

VOCABULARY: ***dentist** – Zahnarzt/-ärztin; **toothache** – Zahnschmerzen; **cold** – Erkältung

12 **Write the answers to complete the dialogue.**

A Why are you late?
B Because [1] I missed the school bus.
A Why did you miss the school bus?
B Because [2] ....
A Why did you get up late?
B Because [3] ....
A Why didn't you hear your alarm clock?
B Because [4] ....
A Why were you so tired?
B Because [5] ....
A Why did you go to bed late?
B Because [6] ....
A Why did you have a lot of homework?
B That's a very good question. Why did you give us so much homework?

SB p. 25

13 Complete the sentences with your own ideas.

1 Sue was happy because ....

2 I didn't go to your party because ....

3 We were angry because ....

4 Henry went to bed early because ....

5 The dog barked because ....

6 Robert didn't go to school because ....

7 The old lady phoned the police because ....

8 Dad went to the supermarket because ....

14 Use your own ideas to write answers to these questions.

1 Why did you buy me this present?
Because I wanted to make you happy.

2 Why did you turn off the TV?
....

3 Why didn't you go to school?
....

4 Why didn't you eat breakfast?
....

5 Why are you so tired today?
....

6 Why haven't you got any money?
....

More Grammar *one / ones*

15 Write mini-dialogues for the pictures. Use the example to help you.

1 try on

A I'd like to try some glasses on.
B Which ones – the red ones or the blue ones?
A The red ones, please.

2 see a film

A ....
B ....
A ....

3 have a pizza

A ....
B ....
A ....

4 borrow

A ....
B ....
A ....

SB p. 25

Developing speaking competencies

16 **Put the dialogue in order.**

☐	**Robin**	It's your laptop. It's broken.
☐	**Robin**	I dropped my cup of coffee on it.
☐	**Robin**	I know. I feel so bad about it.
☐	**Robin**	I'm really sorry.
1	**Robin**	Jay. Erm. I've got something to tell you.
☐	**Jay**	You dropped your coffee on it. You fool.
☐	**Jay**	What!? It's broken?
☐	**Jay**	What is it?
6	**Jay**	But how could you do that?

MORE Words and Phrases

1	**a few**	*A few friends came to my party.*	einige, ein paar
	chocolates	*I had a box of chocolates for my birthday.*	Pralinen
	confused	*He was confused by all the different notices.*	verwirrt
	embarrassed	*She was embarrassed by her silly mistake.*	verlegen
	explain	*I don't understand – can you explain, please?*	erklären
	luckily	*Luckily we arrived in time to see the film.*	glücklicherweise
	operation	*The operation was a great success.*	Operation
	organise	*I want to organise a party for next weekend.*	organisieren
	out loud	*The situation was so funny I laughed out loud.*	laut(hals)
	plan	*We're planning a party for Saturday evening.*	planen
	say sorry	*That was a big mistake – you have to say sorry!*	sich entschuldigen
	success	*The party was a great success.*	Erfolg
	upset	*Please don't be upset – it was a silly mistake.*	böse, verärgert
	be worried	*John didn't come home – his mum is worried.*	sich Sorgen machen
2	sculpture	*There are lots of sculptures in the museum.*	Skulptur
6	**anyone**	*Hello! Is anyone there?*	jemand
	because of	*We didn't go to the beach because of the rain.*	wegen, infolge, aufgrund
	behaviour	*His behaviour at the party was very strange.*	Benehmen, Verhalten
	bully	*Don't let anyone bully you on the internet!*	tyrannisieren, mobben
	go wrong	*Everything is fine – nothing can go wrong!*	schief gehen
	not only ... but also	*His dad has not only a car, but also two motorbikes.*	nicht nur … sondern auch
	pass on	*She passed on the message to her mum.*	weitergeben
	password	*Don't tell anyone your password!*	Passwort
	such	*The party was such a surprise.*	solch, so (ein)
	tip	*I don't know how to use this machine. Can you give me a tip?*	Tipp
	turn up	*Twenty people turned up to my party last week.*	auftauchen
	what sort of	*What sort of food do you like?*	welche Art (von)
8	**awesome**	*The film on TV yesterday was awesome!*	beeindruckend
	confusing	*I think the rules are very confusing!*	verwirrend
	difficult	*I don't think the text is difficult. Do you?*	schwierig
	exciting	*There's an exciting film on TV this evening.*	spannend
	funny	*That was funny. I laughed a lot.*	komisch, witzig

SB p. 26

UNIT 4 Halloween

Essential Vocabulary

1 Write the words under the pictures.

a haunted castle
a candle
knock on a door
a vampire
a witch
cut off the top
a scary face
a pumpkin

1 .... 2 .... 3 ....

4 .... 5 ....

6 .... 7 .... 8 ....

2 Read and complete. Use the words or phrases from 1. Sometimes you need to change the form.

1 **A** Look, there are two big orange balls in grandma's garden.
B Don't be silly. They are
....

2 **A** It's very dark in here.
B OK, I can get a ....

3 **A** Do all .... wear funny hats?
B Yes, they do and they can fly.

4 **A** Don't open the door.
B Why not?
A There's a man with a
.... outside.

5 **A** I don't want to go in there.
B Why not?
A Because it's a ....

6 **A** Don't ....
B Why not?
A Because I've got a key.

7 **A** Please give me the knife.
B What for?
A I want to .... of the pumpkin.

8 **A** I've got my .... costume, but I can't find my plastic teeth.
B They are on the table.

SB p. 28, 29

More Vocabulary

3 Do the crossword.

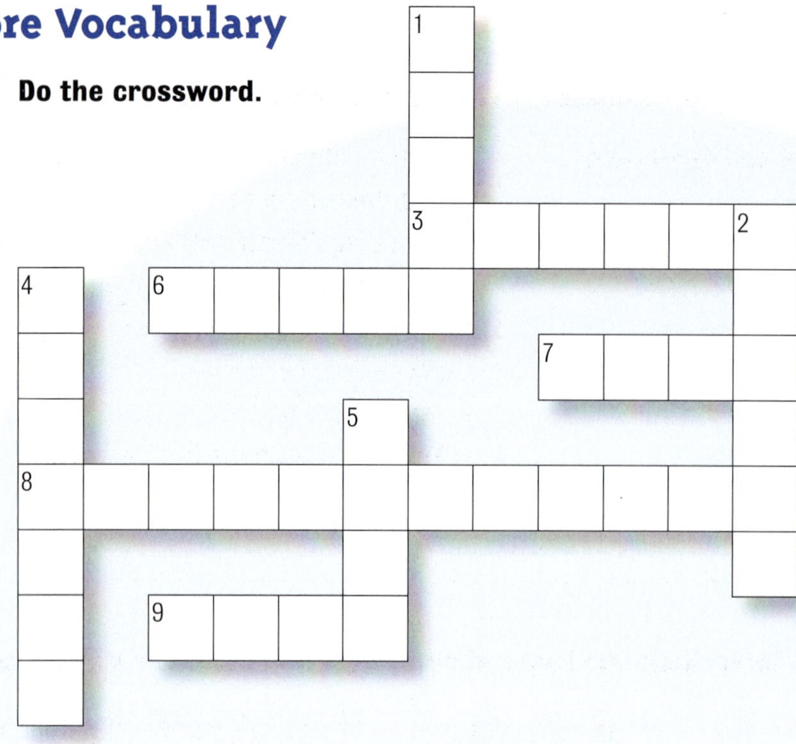

DOWN:

1 

2 

4 You wear it at a Halloween party.

5 

ACROSS:

3 

6 The opposite of child.

7 

8 That's what you say at Halloween.

9 

4 Complete with the correct form of the words and phrases from 3.

Last Halloween I went [1].. with my friends.
We put on our scary [2].. and our Halloween
[3].. .
First we went down our street. We knocked at the door of Mrs Jones.
An [4].. opened. I didn't know him. "Where's
Mrs Jones?" I said. The man smiled. Suddenly I heard a noise. There was a [5].. .
We ran away. "Come back," she shouted. It was Mrs Jones. We went back and she gave us lots of
[6].. .

Then we went to the old house at the end of the street. We opened the
[7].. and went up the [8].. .
We knocked. Nobody opened. We knocked again. "There's nobody there,"
I said. "Look at the window," said my friend. "I can see a light." "Let's put
superglue in the [9]..," my friend said.
"Look at the window," I shouted. There was a word in big red letters in
the window. The word was: Danger*!
We ran.

VOCABULARY: *danger – Gefahr

SB p. 29, 30

Reading and Writing

5 Match the sentence halves for a summary of the story *Trick or treat*.

1 Last Halloween Larry and Kerry went
2 There they met a
3 Together they went to an old house. It
4 An old man opened the door and
5 Jim wanted to play a trick
6 Suddenly the door opened, then it
7 Larry and Kerry went home and
8 The chief inspector told

☐ on the old man. He put superglue into the lock.
☐ told their parents and the police.
☐ closed again and Jim wasn't there any more.
☐ trick-or-treating on the other side of the town.
☐ them: "The house has been empty for 20 years."
☐ boy. His name was Jim.
☐ said: "Go away."
☐ looked like a house from a horror film.

6 CHOICES

A Halloween – 20 years later. Read the text and put the pictures into the correct order.

1 Twenty years later my brother Larry and I went to the house again. "Let's knock on the door," Larry said to me.
2 We went up to the house, but I was a bit scared.
3 Larry laughed at me and knocked. Nothing happened. We started to walk away.
4 Then a man came out of the house. He looked like Jim, but twenty years older.
5 "At last you are here," he said. "Come in, come in." And he took my brother by the hand.
6 I shouted and pulled Larry away. Then we ran.
7 We heard a very loud sigh* coming from the house.
8 Then the house collapsed*.

VOCABULARY
***sigh** – Seufzer;
collapse – einstürzen

SB p. 30

B **Look at the pictures. Then write the story. Use the words in the box below to help you.**

One Halloween, two children knocked on the door …
An old woman …
She looked like …
The children said: " …
The old woman said: " …
She went back …
After some minutes, she …
Behind her were …
They laughed and shouted …
The children …

....
....
....
....
....
....
....
....
....

7 **Complete the dialogue with the sentences in the box. There are three sentences that you do not need.**

And don't stay out very late.
Can we go now, Mum?
Have we got another black hat?
Thanks, Mum.
That's a lot of chocolate.
Trick or treat, Aunt Melinda.
Yes, I've got it, Mum. Can we go now?

Mum Let me look at you. Oh, great! You look nice and scary!
Allie Thanks, Mum. 1 ....
Mum Yes, but be careful. Always stay with Jimmy.
Allie I know, Mum.
Jimmy Yeah, Mum, we know. Don't worry.
Mum 2 ....
Jimmy Until ten. Is that OK?
Mum OK. And have you got your mobile?
Allie 3 ....
Mum Yes, of course. Have fun.
Jimmy 4 ....
Allie Bye, Mum!
Mum And Jimmy? Have you got the bag for the sweets?
Jimmy Oh, Mum!

SB p. 30

Essential Grammar *should – shouldn't*

8 Write the sentences under the pictures.

She should see a doctor.
He should go to bed.
He shouldn't drive so fast.
He shouldn't go in there.
He shouldn't eat so much.
He should invite her to the cinema.

1 ....

2 ....

3 ....

4 ....

5 ....

6 ....

9 Match the dialogues.

1 I'm scared at Halloween.	☐	You shouldn't go to bed so late.
2 I'm tired.	☐	You should take an umbrella.
3 I'm hungry.	☐	You should say you're sorry.
4 My head hurts.	☐	You should take it to the vet*.
5 My mum's angry with me.	☐	You should take an aspirin.
6 My cat's ill.	☐	You shouldn't leave the house then.
7 It's raining outside.	☐	You shouldn't watch it alone.
8 It's a very scary film.	☐	You should eat an apple.

VOCABULARY
***vet** – Tierarzt/-ärztin

10 Here is what parents say to their kids at Halloween. Write *should* or *shouldn't*.

1 You .... say thank you when you get a treat.
2 You .... scare very small kids.
3 You .... go into houses of people you don't know.
4 You .... eat too many sweets.
5 You .... take your mobile with you.
6 You .... stay out too long.

SB p. 31

More Grammar *should – shouldn't*

11 Write *should* or *shouldn't* to complete the speech bubbles.

1

2

3

4

5

6

12 Use the verbs in the box to complete the letter.

buy
visit
go
speak
bring
go
eat
try
take

Hi Paulo,

I'm so happy about your visit next week. It's your first visit to my country, so here's some advice for you.

The weather is quite cold, so you should ¹.......................... some warm clothes. You shouldn't ².......................... them here because they are very expensive.

To get to my house you should ³.......................... the train. It's only 20 minutes from the airport. You shouldn't ⁴.......................... by taxi because (again) it's very expensive.

When you are here, you should ⁵.......................... the museum and the castle. They are very interesting. You should also ⁶.......................... to see a musical – it's fantastic! You should definitely ⁷.......................... some of the local food – it's delicious. There are lots of great restaurants here and they are quite cheap. You shouldn't ⁸.......................... at the fast food restaurants though. They're just the same as the ones in your country. Finally, you should ⁹.......................... to some local people. It's a great way to practise your English.

I hope you enjoy your stay. I can't wait to see you.

Love, Ally

13 What should visitors to your town do or not do? Write some suggestions.

When you come to my town, you should:

- ....
- ....
- ....
- ....

When you come to my town, you shouldn't:

- ....
- ....
- ....
- ....

SB p. 32

WORD FILE

Halloween

In a haunted castle

MORE Words and Phrases

2	**brave**	*When he went to hospital, he was very brave.*	tapfer
	fear	*We don't fear ghosts or monsters!*	(sich) fürchten (vor)
3	**aged (11)**	*John and Peter are two boys aged eleven.*	(11) Jahre alt
	play a trick	*They played a trick on the old man.*	einen Streich spielen
	stairs	*John went up the stairs to his bedroom.*	Stiege
	tradition	*Trick-or-treating is a tradition at Halloween.*	Tradition
4	**awful**	*That film on TV last night was awful!*	schrecklich
	knife	*Use a knife to cut the cake.*	Messer
	sound	*Please be quiet and don't make a sound.*	Geräusch
5	**age**	*They are the same age.*	Alter
	(door) lock	*I turned the key in the lock and opened the door.*	(Tür-)Schloss
	mean	*Don't be so mean – let me ride your bike!*	gemein
	should	*It's Sally's birthday – we should get her a present.*	sollte/n, solltest
	side	*John lives on the other side of the street.*	Seite
	twin	*These two boys are twins.*	Zwilling; Zwillings-
9	**disappear**	*Come back soon – don't disappear!*	verschwinden
12	**plenty of**	*Last Halloween, my neighbour gave me plenty of sweets.*	eine Menge von
13	keen (on)	*I'm not so keen on Maths.*	begeistert (von)
	kick	*Ouch! That was a hard kick!*	Tritt, Stoß

SWYK Units 1–4

UNIT 5 Amazing animals

Essential Vocabulary

1 Write the words under the pictures.

pig
dolphin
antelope
mosquito
anaconda
chimpanzee
giraffe
cheetah
whale
rhino
ostrich
crocodile

1 ....

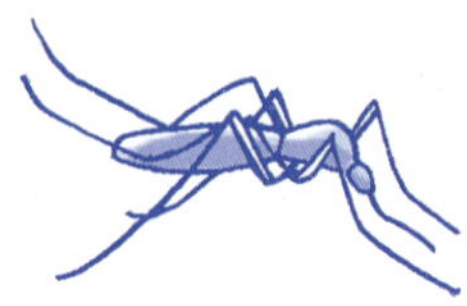

2 ....

3 ....

4 ....

5 ....

6 ....

7 ....

8 ....

9 ....

10 ....

11 ....

12 ....

2 Write the adjectives under the pictures.

strong
heavy
friendly
big
small
dangerous
hairy
clever

1 ....

2 ....

3 ....

4 ....

5 ....

6 ....

7 ....

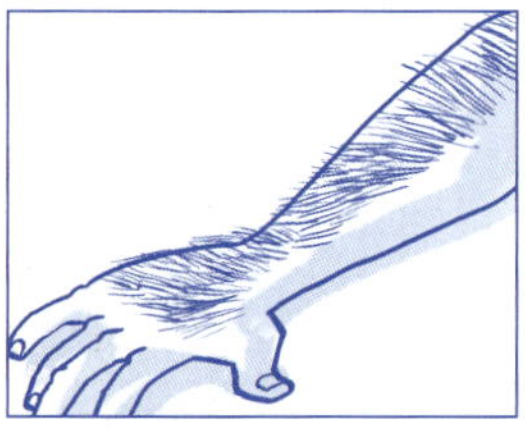

8 ....

SB p. 34, 36, 37

More Vocabulary

3 Write down some of the animals from 1.

1 These animals are very fast: ....
2 These animals are very tall: ....
3 These animals are very dangerous: ....
4 These animals are very heavy: ....
5 These animals are very long: ....

Reading and Writing

4 Complete the summary of the story *Saved by a pig*. Write *Bacon*, *Judith* or *Jeff*.

Judith Crowe, her son Jeff and his pet pig Bacon went swimming in the river on a hot day. [1]........................ was only five years old and his pet pig was better at swimming than him.
They played and swam for an hour. Then [2]........................ got out of the water. [3]........................ swam into the middle of the river, where the water was deeper and more dangerous. He was in trouble.

[4]........................ jumped into the water and tried to swim to her son. But [5]........................ was faster than her and got to the boy first.
[6]........................ put his arms round the pig. But he was bigger and heavier than [7]........................ . They went under the water. But suddenly [8]........................ saw [9]........................ come out of the water on [10]........................'s back! She was very happy.

5 CHOICES

A Read the texts on p. 35 of the Student's Book again and write the names of the animals.

Ruckle
Bugboy
Snapkle
Hipcop

1 It was as big as a rabbit. ....
2 It was as big as an elephant. ....
3 It was as dangerous as a snake. ....
4 It was as clever as a chimpanzee. ....
5 It was as poisonous as the blue-ringed octopus. ....
6 It wasn't as beautiful as an elephant. ....
7 It was as small as a mouse. ....

B Put the text about animals in Atlantis in the correct order.

☐ a lot. Their favourite pet was the Ruckle – it was half
☐ as the Hipcop. There were other animals that the Atlantians
1 The people who lived in Atlantis liked animals
☐ land animal and half bird, but it didn't fly. The Ruckle
☐ didn't keep as pets. One of them was a small
☐ very beautiful, but it wasn't as ugly as the Snapkle.
☐ dangerous – as dangerous as a blue-ringed octopus. It wasn't
☐ reptile called the Bugboy. The Bugboy was very, very
☐ was friendlier than the Hipcop, but it wasn't as clever

6 **Read the text. How many of the tasks below can you do?**

Ricky's safari trip

Last year we went on safari to Africa. It was great – we saw lots of brilliant birds and animals. I really liked the rhino that we saw one day – it was very big (about 1.5m high) and I'm sure it was really heavy, too. The guide* said that sometimes a rhino can weigh 2,000 kilograms! But I wasn't scared. My dad told me that rhinos aren't very dangerous animals. Rhinos are almost blind and so they can't see well. There were lots of small grey and white birds on the rhinoceros' back. I think the birds eat very small insects from the rhino's skin*.

Later the same day we saw some baboons*. There was a big family of them. I thought they looked nice and friendly, but we didn't go very close. You have to be careful, because male* baboons are strong and they aren't very friendly! Some people think baboons are very intelligent, too. I don't know about that, but I'm sure they're more intelligent than rhinos!

At the end of the day, when we went back to the hotel – guess what? In my parents' room there was a big, black, hairy tarantula*! My dad was really scared, but my mum just picked it up and put it outside. My mum's really cool!

VOCABULARY: ***guide** – Führer; **skin** – Haut; **baboon** – Pavian; **male** – männlich; **tarantula** – Tarantel

Circle T (*True*) or F (*False*).

1 Ricky really liked the spider. T / F
2 The rhino was more than 2 metres tall. T / F
3 Rhinos are not very dangerous. T / F

Choose the correct answer.

4 What was on the rhino's back? ☐ birds ☐ insects ☐ small mice
5 What was the second animal Ricky saw? ☐ rhinos ☐ baboons ☐ spiders
6 Why is it not a good idea to go too close to baboons?
☐ they take your food ☐ they are shy ☐ they are dangerous

Answer the questions.

7 Why did Ricky not get nervous when they were close to a rhino? ....
8 Where was the spider? ....
9 What did Ricky's mum do with the spider? ....

7 **Check your answers.**

SB p. 37

8 **Complete the sentences with the words in the box.**

desert mosquito weigh cheetah whale worldwide poisonous Thailand

1 The taipan is a very .... snake.

2 The Sahara is a very big .... in Africa.

3 A .... can give you malaria.

4 Some rhinos .... about 2,000 kilos!

5 More than two billion people .... speak English.

6 The .... is the biggest mammal in the sea.

7 Bumblebee bats live in ....

8 No animal in the world is faster than the ....

Essential Grammar Comparatives

9 **Complete with the comparative form of the adjectives in brackets.**

1 **A** The pizza at Tony's is .... (good) than the pizza at Little Italy.
B You're right.

2 **A** It's very hot today.
B Yes, but it was much .... (hot) yesterday.

3 **A** My bag is .... (heavy) than yours.
B Well, I'm not carrying so many books around.

4 **A** A Ferrari is .... (fast) than a Porsche.
B True, and it's .... (expensive) than a Porsche.

5 **A** How much .... (old) than you is your brother?
B Three years. He was fifteen in June.

Essential Grammar *as ... as*

10 **Complete B's answers. Use the same adjective as A.**

1 **A** I don't think squash is exciting.
B Really? I think ...*it's as exciting as*.. tennis.

2 **A** I don't think rabbits are interesting.
B Really? I think .... hamsters.

3 **A** I don't think spiders are scary.
B Really? I think .... snakes.

4 **A** I don't think your dog is clever.
B Really? I think .... your cat!

5 **A** I don't think this DVD is good.
B Really? I think .... the other one.

6 **A** I don't think you're very strong.
B Really? I think .... you!

SB p. 35, 36

Essential Grammar Comparatives / Superlatives

11 **Circle the correct word.**

1 Ostriches are *faster* / *fastest* than people.
2 The taipan is the *poisonous* / *most poisonous* snake in the world.
3 The anaconda is the *longer* / *longest* snake in the world.
4 This book about animals is the *best* / *better*.
5 Gorillas are *bigger* / *biggest* than chimpanzees.
6 Cheetahs are *fastest* / *faster* than rhinos.
7 The Snapkle was the *ugliest* / *ugly* animal in Atlantis.
8 The Ruckle was the *most popular* / *popular* pet.

More Grammar Comparatives

12 **Write sentences comparing the animals. You can use the adjectives from the box. Use a different adjective for each picture.**

beautiful
strong
fast
~~big~~
funny
dangerous
scary
small

1 Elephants are bigger than rhinos.

2 ....

3 ....

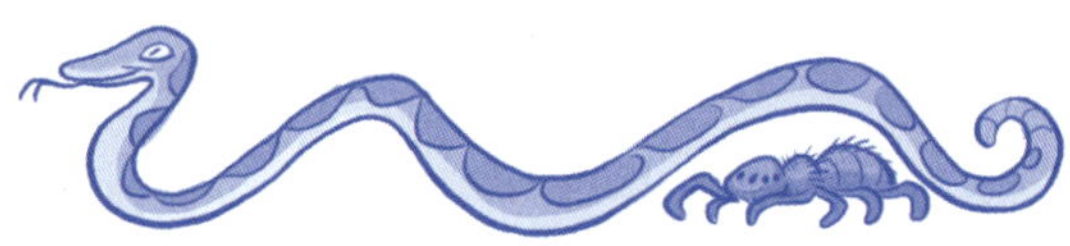

4 ....

5 ....

6 ....

More Grammar *as ... as / Comparatives*

13 **Read the sentences. Tick the ones you think are true.**

1 The Eiffel Tower isn't as tall as the Empire State Building. ☐
2 The River Nile isn't as long as the River Amazon. ☐
3 There aren't as many people in Switzerland* as in Austria. ☐
4 There aren't as many lakes in Finland as in Germany. ☐
5 The blue-ringed octopus isn't as dangerous as the mosquito. ☐
6 The Estuarine crocodile isn't as long as the taipan. ☐
7 Elephants aren't as heavy as blue whales. ☐
8 Austria isn't as big as Hungary. ☐

VOCABULARY
***Switzerland** – Schweiz

SB p. 35, 36, 37

14 Complete the text. Use *as … as* or comparative adjectives.

A I see you've got all the Harry Potter books. What do you think of them?

B I really like all the Harry Potter books. I've read them all. I think that *The Chamber of Secrets* is a 1 .... (good) book than *The Order of the Phoenix. The Chamber of Secrets* is 2 .... (interesting) and 3 .... (exciting) than *The Order of the Phoenix.* And *The Order of the Phoenix* is much 4 .... (long).

A What do you think of the films?

B Well, *The Philosopher's Stone* film isn't 5 .... (good) the book. I really like the books much 6 .... (good) than the films.

A Tell me more about the books.

B Well, *The Goblet of Fire* was 7 .... (good) than *The Chamber of Secrets*. And *The Chamber of Secrets* was 8 .... (exciting) than *The Prisoner of Azkaban.*

A So what should I read?

B Start at the beginning with *The Philosopher's Stone*, of course.

15 Write sentences comparing Ronnie and Reggie. Use *as … as* or comparative adjectives.

tall
clever
old
heavy
fast

	date of birth	weight*	height*	school report	time for 100m
Ronnie	March 22nd 2005	50kg	1.56m	A+	18 seconds
Reggie	March 22nd 2005	52kg	1.56m	C-	16 seconds

....

....

....

....

....

More Grammar Superlatives

16 Harry, Larry and Barry are brothers – triplets*! Look at the picture and the table and write sentences. Use the adjectives in the box.

~~tall~~
old
heavy
intelligent
short
young
slow
fast

	Harry	Barry	Larry
date of birth	02/02/05 10.20 a.m.	02/02/05 10.50 a.m.	02/02/05 11.40 a.m.
school report	All 'C's	All 'B's	All 'A's
weight	47kg	43kg	53kg
running 100m	12.5 seconds	18 seconds	14.6 seconds

Harry is the tallest. ....

....

....

....

VOCABULARY: ***weight** – Gewicht; **height** – Größe; **triplets** – Drillinge

SB p. 39

17 Answer the questions for you.

1 Who is the tallest person in your family?

....

2 What is the best thing in your bedroom?

....

3 What is the heaviest thing in your house or flat?

....

4 What is the most expensive thing in your house?

....

5 What is the most interesting animal in the world?

....

6 What is your best subject at school?

....

WORD FILE

More animals

SB p. 39

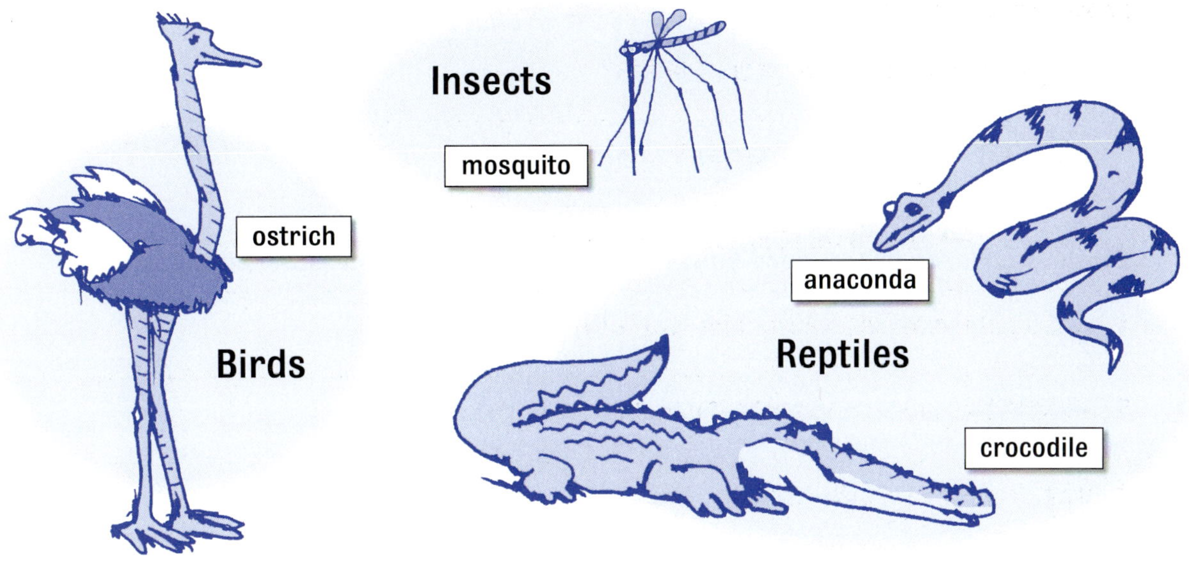

MORE Words and Phrases

1	**all the time**	*It rains all the time in winter.*	die ganze Zeit
	deep	*The water is deep there.*	tief
	disappear	*The chimpanzee ran away and disappeared in a tree.*	verschwinden
	heavy	*This bag is a bit heavy.*	schwer
	in trouble	*He was in trouble – he couldn't swim!*	in Schwierigkeiten
	middle	*This towel is wet in the middle.*	Mitte
	safe	*Is it safe to swim here?*	sicher
	swimmer	*She is an amazing swimmer.*	Schwimmer/in
	towel	*Have you got a dry towel?*	Handtuch
	turn around	*When she turned around, she saw the pig.*	(sich) umdrehen
6	**friendly**	*Dolphins are friendly animals.*	freundlich
	mountain	*Were there mountains in Atlantis?*	Berg
	popular	*They are friendly and popular.*	beliebt
	ugly	*The rhino is an ugly animal.*	hässlich
10	**carry**	*Mosquitoes can carry malaria.*	tragen; hier: übertragen
	desert	*There are no deserts in England.*	Wüste
	die	*Millions of people die from malaria.*	sterben
	gram	*How many grams are there in a ton?*	Gramm
	mammal	*Elephants and lions are mammals.*	Säugetier
	South East Asia	*The crocodiles of South East Asia are the longest in the world.*	Südostasien
	ton	*The helicopter can lift a ton very easily.*	Tonne (1000 Kilo)
	weigh	*I weigh about 60 kilos.*	wiegen
14	**almost**	*The blue whale weighs almost 150,000 kilos.*	fast
	grow	*The crocodile can grow to eight metres.*	wachsen
	high	*The giraffe is the tallest animal at nearly six metres high.*	hoch; groß
	nearly	*Come on, Susan! It's nearly three o'clock!*	fast, beinahe
15	**cup**	*I'd like a cup of tea, please.*	Tasse
G	**fat**	*My dog's too fat; he needs exercise.*	fett
	simple	*Juggling with two balls is simple.*	einfach
DVD	It depends.		Es kommt darauf an.

UNIT 6 Where's the post office?

Essential Vocabulary

1 Circle the words in the word snake. Then write them under the pictures.

1 ....

2 ....

3 ....

10 ....

9 ....

8 ....

4 ....

5 ....

6 ....

7 ....

2 Write the words or phrases under the pictures.

take the second left
opposite
go through the park
turn right
cross the bridge
go straight ahead
go past the traffic lights

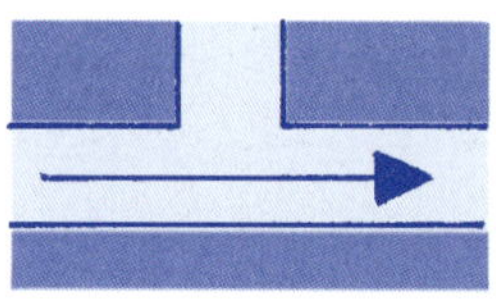

1 ....

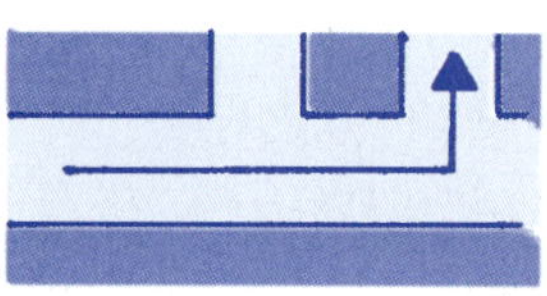

2 ....

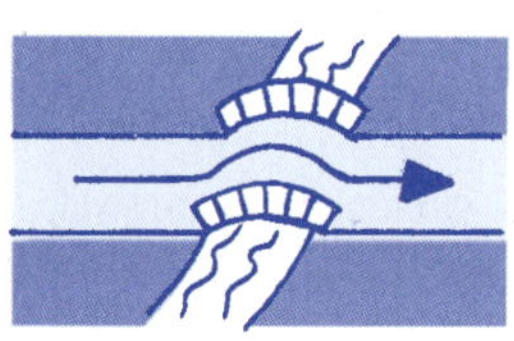

3 ....

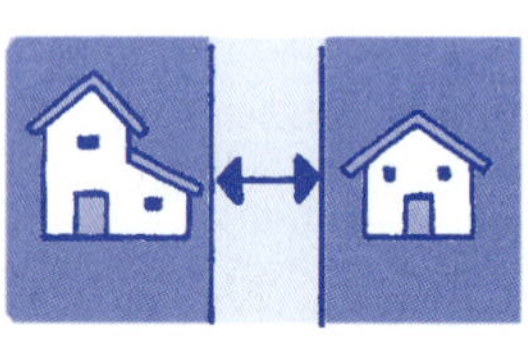

4 ....

5 ....

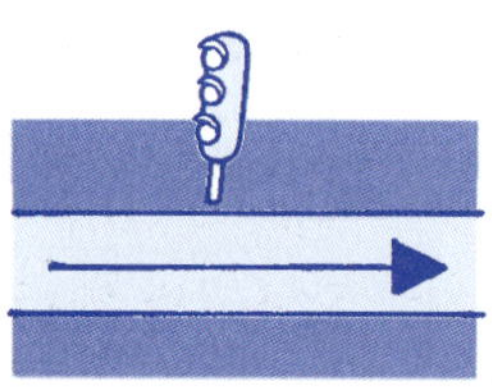

6 ....

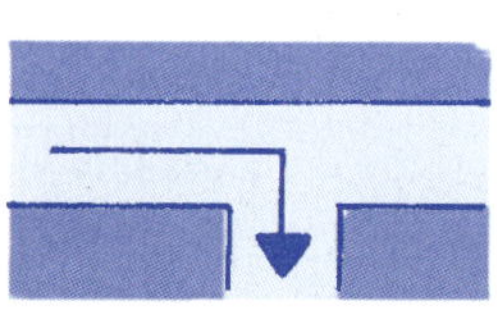

7 ....

SB p. 42, 43

More Vocabulary

3 Where are these people going? Choose from the words in the box.

railway station
police station
post office
tourist office
bank
church
hospital
~~shopping centre~~

1 They're going to the shopping centre. ....

2 ....

3 ....

4 ....

5 ....

6 ....

7 ....

8 ....

Reading and Writing

4 Complete the dialogues with four of the sentences in the box. There are two extra sentences in the box.

Do you see the traffic lights* up there?

Go past the post office and turn left.

Right, straight ahead, then left.

The bank's just round the corner there.

The church is behind the bank.

Where's that?

DIALOGUE 1

Girl Excuse me, I'm looking for a bank.
Woman That's easy. Go as far as the shopping centre …
Girl [1] ....
Woman Just follow this road. It's on your left. At the shopping centre turn right …
Girl OK, right at the shopping centre.
Woman [2] ....
Girl Thank you.
Woman You're welcome.

DIALOGUE 2

Man Excuse me, can you tell me the way to the post office?
Woman The post office? Hmm. There's one in Maple Road.
Man Maple Road? How do I get there?
Woman [3] ....
Man Yes …
Woman Go to the traffic lights, turn right, go straight ahead and then turn left.
Man [4] ....
Woman That's Maple Road. The post office is right in front of you.
Man Thank you.

SB p. 43, 45

5 CHOICES

Look at the map of Edinburgh. Read text A or B and draw the routes on your map. Find out where you are going.

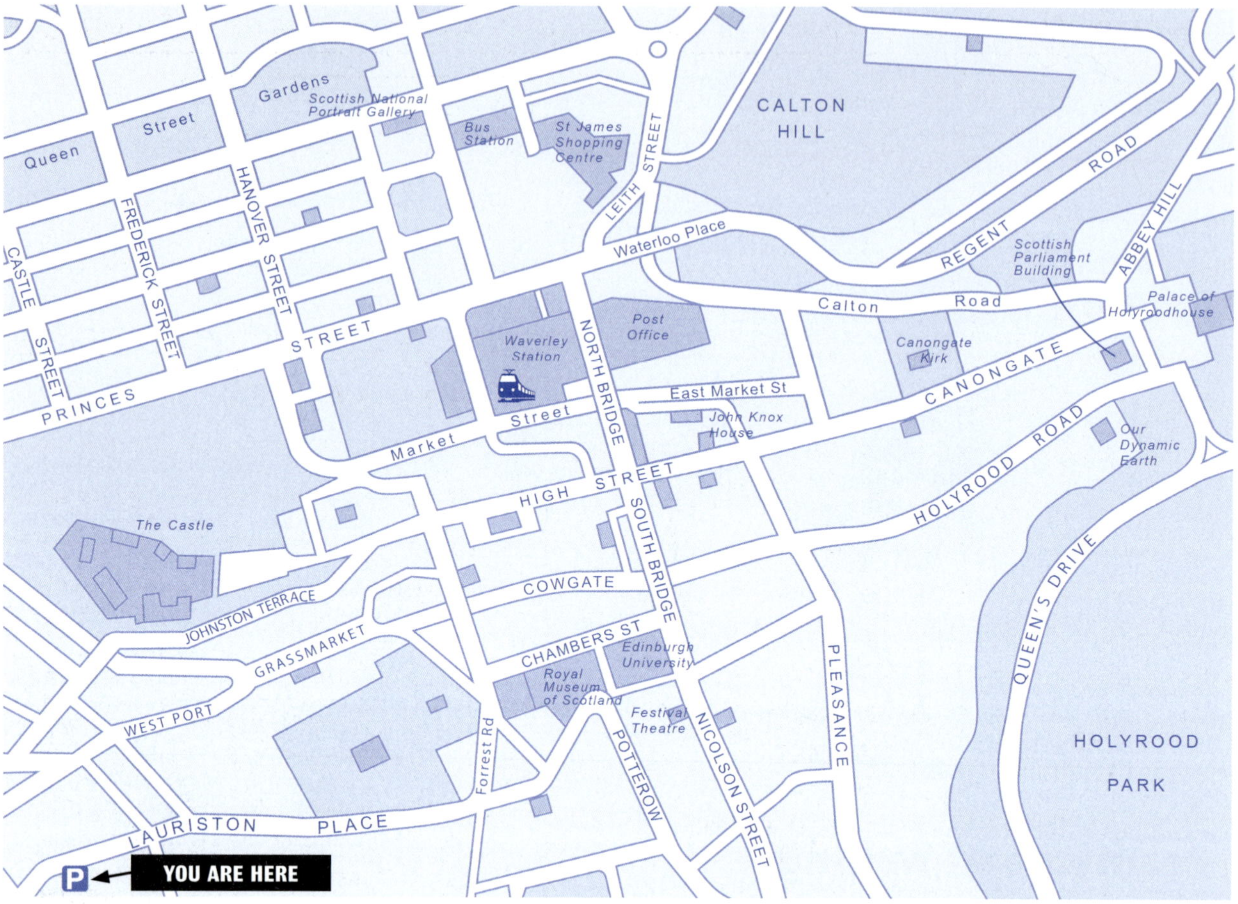

A

Go out of the car park and turn right into Lauriston Place. Walk along Lauriston Place. Turn left into Forrest Road and then take the second right. At the end of Chambers Street turn left into South Bridge. Go straight ahead. At the end of North Bridge there's .... opposite the post office.

B

Go out of the car park and turn right. At the end of Lauriston Place turn right into Potterow. Follow it and then take the first small lane to the left. When you get to Pleasance, turn left. At the corner of Pleasance and High Street turn right. Go past Canongate Kirk and the Scottish Parliament Building. At the end of Canongate there's the ....*

VOCABULARY: *lane – Gasse

SB p. 44

6 **Work in pairs. Student B works with the map here. Student A works with the map on page 44 in the Student's Book. Student B asks Student A for the way to the post office, the cinema, the supermarket, the church.**

B Excuse me, how do I get to … / Excuse me, I'm trying to find … / Excuse me, I'm looking for … ?

A That's easy. Take the …

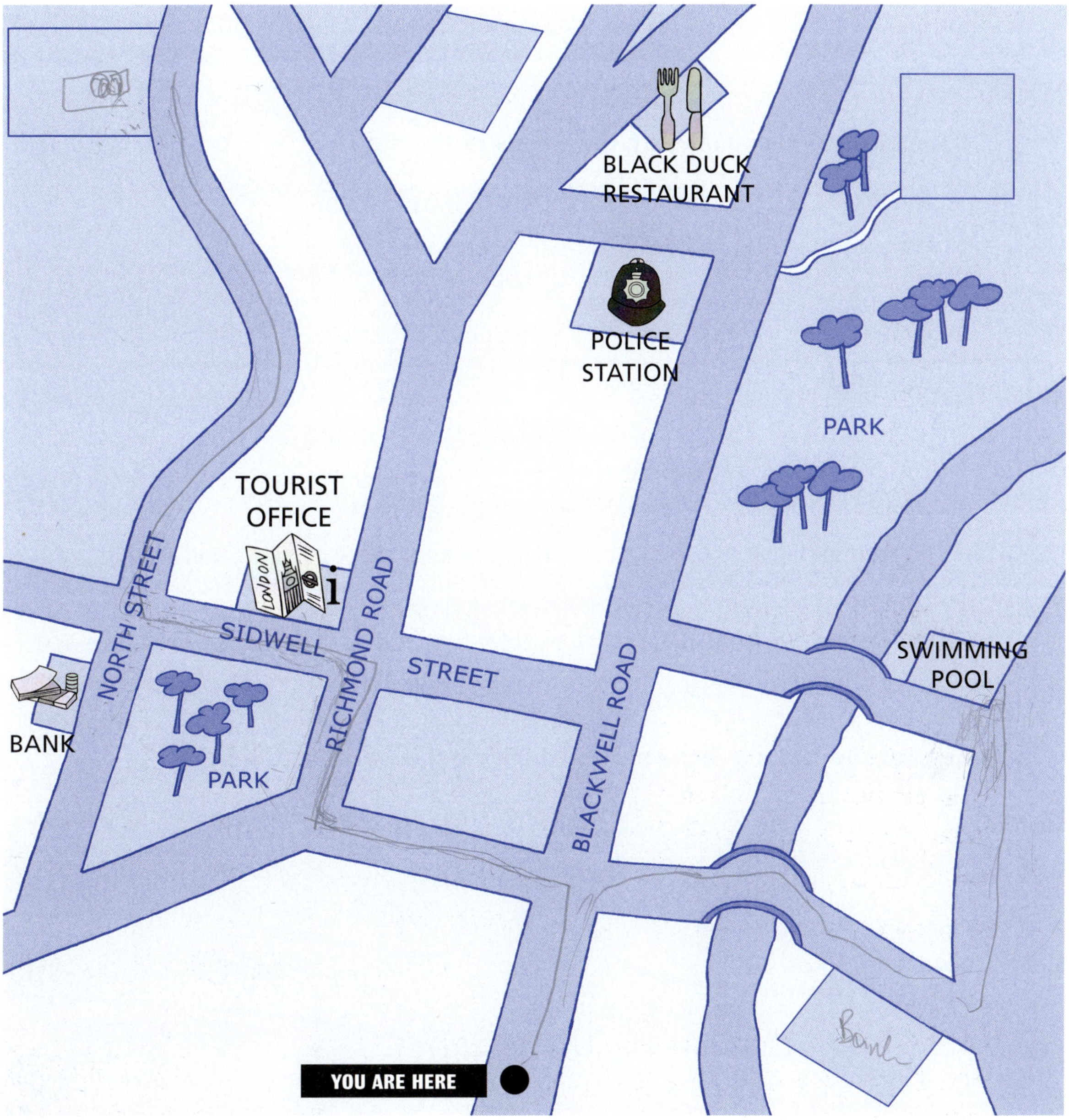

7 **Write a text explaining the way from your home to one of the places below.**

the (nearest) church	the (nearest) cinema	your school
the (nearest) bus station	the (nearest) post office	your favourite shop
the (nearest) supermarket		

....

....

....

....

SB p. 44

Essential Grammar Directions (Prepositions of place)

8 Read the dialogue and circle the correct answer.

A Excuse me? How do I get to the railway station?

B The railway station? OK. Go [1] *straight down / left* this road. Go [2] *until / as far as* the large supermarket on your left. OK? After the supermarket, [3] *go / take* the second on the right. After about 20 metres, turn [4] *ahead / right* again. Go [5] *past / down* the post office, turn [6] *on / right* at the Station Hotel and there, in front of you, is the railway station. It's a twenty-minute walk.

A Thanks.

B No problem.

9 Complete the dialogues with the words in the box.

cross
ahead
~~straight~~
right
second
turn
take
far

1 **Tourist** Excuse me, where's the railway station?
Policeman Go ....straight.... ahead and take the .... right.

2 **Bank robber** Excuse me, where's the nearest bank?
Policeman .... the street and go as .... as the cinema. The bank is next door.

3 **Man** Excuse me, where's the nearest post office?
Policeman .... left, go as far as the cinema and turn ....

4 **Tourist** Excuse me, where's the Chelsea Hotel?
Policeman Go straight .... Go past the shopping centre and .... the first right.

10 Look at the picture. Write sentences using the words in the box.

next to
behind
opposite
in front of
on the corner of

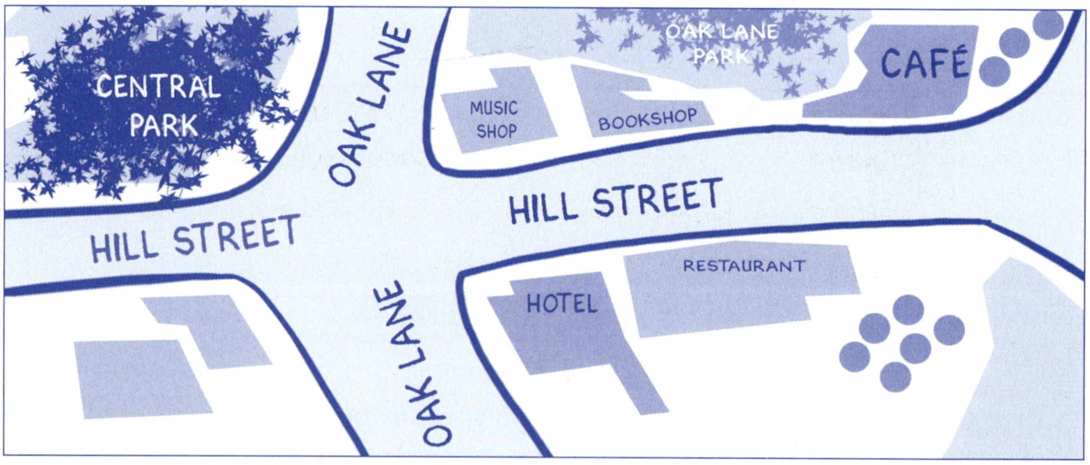

Start like this:

On the corner of Hill Street and Oak Lane there's a music shop. Next to ...

....

....

....

SB p. 43, 47

11 Put the words in order to give directions.

1 straight / go / ahead

....

2 the / left / take / second

....

3 past / right / the / go / turn / park / and

....

4 the / left / cinema / on / the / is

....

5 there / bank / the / is / over

....

6 the / as / as / post / go / office / far

....

7 tourist / right / the / office / turn / at

....

Developing speaking competencies

12 Complete the mini dialogues.

Man [1]E............................ m............................ .
Woman Yes?
Man Have you got the time?
Woman Yes, it's 4.45.
Man [2]S............................ ?
Woman It's a quarter to five.
Man Thank you.

Woman I'm [3]s............................ t............................ b............................ y............................ , but when's the next bus?
Man The next bus is in half an hour.
Woman [4]S............................ t............................ at half past four?
Man Yes, that's right.

13 Put the dialogue in the correct order.

☐ **Tourist** So that's past the lights, second right and the tourist office is on the left.
☐ **Tourist** I'm sorry to bother you, but can you tell me where the tourist office is?
1 **Tourist** Excuse me?
☐ **Tourist** Thank you.
☐ **Tourist** Yes, I can.
☐ **Tourist** Sorry?
☐ **Policeman** The tourist office. Let me think. Can you see the traffic lights over there?
☐ **Policeman** You're welcome.
6 **Policeman** Go past the lights and take the second right …
☐ **Policeman** Go past the lights and take the second right and the tourist office is on the left.
☐ **Policeman** Yes?
☐ **Policeman** That's right.

WORD FILE

In a town

How do I get there?

MORE Words and Phrases

1	**forest**	*There are lots of tall trees in the forest.*	Wald
	hill	*Walk up the hill as far as the church.*	Hügel
	luck	*Good luck, sir!*	Glück
	path	*This is the best path through the forest.*	Weg, Pfad
3	**map**	*You can see where we are on the map.*	Karte
	(not) at all	*Thank you. – Not at all.*	gar nicht; hier: keine Ursache
4	**as far as**	*Follow the road as far as the supermarket.*	bis zu
5	**directions**	*Can you give me directions on how to get to the station?*	Anweisungen
6	**change trains**	*We have to change trains at Waterloo Station.*	umsteigen
	cover	*There's a nice picture on the cover of this book.*	Umschlag; hier: Titelseite
	missing	*His dog was missing for three days.*	vermisst
	most of the time	*In the forest it rains most of the time.*	meistens
	pocket	*He put his ticket into his coat pocket.*	Tasche (bei Kleidungsstück)
	safe and well	*Everyone is happy now he is safe and well.*	gesund und wohlbehalten
	too	*It's too dangerous to go into the forest at night.*	zu

UNIT 7 Outdoor adventure

Essential Vocabulary

1 Write the numbers next to the words.

- ☐ field
- ☐ moon
- ☐ forest
- ☐ valley
- ☐ mountains
- ☐ beach
- ☐ town
- ☐ waterfall
- ☐ sea
- ☐ village
- ☐ hill
- ☐ road
- ☐ stars
- ☐ river
- ☐ lake

2 Match the pictures with the sentences.

1 They're canoeing on a river.
2 They're swimming next to a waterfall.
3 They're having a picnic.
4 They're rock climbing.
5 They're building a tree house.
6 They're geo-caching.

SB p. 50, 51

More Vocabulary

3 Write the words.

oeg-ghcniac	geo-caching	vglaeli	....	tferso	....
wont	....	kale	....	duieg	....
awtmroyo	....	laeafrtlw	....	ampc	....
droa	....	ccinip	....	gnthi	....
dfilse	....	uns	....	rtssa	....
elalvy	....	noitaunm	....	nomo	....
ievrr	....	SGP tinu	....		

Reading and Writing

4 Read the story. How many of the tasks below can you do?

Jeremy and Scott were best friends. One day Jeremy said, "Let's go geo-caching next weekend." Scott loved the idea. On Friday, they put some food and some orange juice in a bag. First Jeremy's dad took them in his car. They left the town and drove on the motorway for twenty minutes before they came to a smaller road. There were beautiful fields on both sides. They drove through a valley, crossed a river, and when they arrived at a little village, the boys got out of the car and said goodbye to Jeremy's dad. They walked for half an hour. Then they came to a lake with a beautiful waterfall. The boys had a picnic.

The sun was very hot, so they drank a lot of the orange juice. Then they took out their GPS unit and started walking towards the mountains. They hoped to find the cache soon. But they just couldn't find it. They walked higher up the mountain and then through a forest for three or four hours. They were tired, hot and hungry. They had very little food and no juice left. Suddenly their GPS unit didn't work any more. The battery was dead! The two friends started to worry. How could they find their way back without their GPS?

They didn't know what to do, and they got very worried. Suddenly they heard some voices. It was a group of kids with their guide. They were from a camp not far away. "It's too late for you to go back now," the guide said. He had a mobile phone and called Jeremy's dad. He was very happy to hear that the boys were safe. Jeremy and Scott stayed at the camp for the night. It was a beautiful night – there were lots of stars and the moon was very bright.

Choose the correct answer.

1 Jeremy and Scott were *brothers / friends*.

2 They got to the village *by car / on foot*.

3 It was a very *warm / cold* day.

Complete the sentences.

4 They walked for a long time and then they felt ....

5 The GPS unit stopped working because the ....

6 They were worried that with no GPS they couldn't ....

Answer the questions.

7 Who did the boys meet up the mountain? ....

8 Why did the guide use his mobile phone? ....

9 How did Jeremy and Scott feel when they came to the camp? ....

5 Check your answers.

SB p. 50, 52, 53

6 CHOICES

A Complete the dialogue with words from the box.

right
tomorrow
picnic area
drink
picnic
bags

A Let's go for a picnic [1].. .

B A [2].. ? Good idea.

A OK, can you bring some sandwiches? I'll bring something to [3].. .

B Sure.

A And can you bring some bags?

B [4].. ? What for?

A We need them. We have to clean up the [5].. after the picnic.

B That's [6].. . Good thinking!

Come along for a picnic

- Friday 2 p.m.
- Bring sandwiches and drinks.
- Bring some bags – clean up the picnic area after the picnic.

B Put the dialogue in the correct order.

Let's go rock climbing

- Tuesday 3 p.m.
- Wear warm clothes and a good pair of boots.
- Wear a hard hat all the time!

☐ A Oh, come on. Everyone's going.
[1] A Let's go rock climbing tomorrow.
☐ A Great. But bring some warm clothes and a good pair of boots*. And you have to wear a hard hat all the time.
☐ B Of course. I know that.
☐ B Rock climbing? I'm not sure.
☐ B Everyone? Oh, alright. I hope it's fun.

VOCABULARY: ***boot** – Stiefel

7 Write similar dialogues for these notices in your exercise book.

Let's go and build a tree house

- Monday 10 a.m.
- Get a hard hat from the office and wear it all the time.

Let's go on a picnic

- Wednesday 1 p.m.
- Bring your own food.
- Free cola and orange juice
- Don't forget to clean up the picnic area after the picnic.

SB p. 51

…e summary of the story *Treasure hunt* on pages 52–53 of the Student's Book. …e four extra sentences. Cross them out.

…vent to an adventure holiday …vith his nine-year-old sister Gillie.

…ought the camp was great.

…rents phoned them every night.

4 The guides were great and Chris especially liked one called Ron.

5 One Wednesday Chris, Gillie and some more kids went geo-caching.

6 Gillie found something in a hole.

7 It wasn't the cache. It was some old coins.

8 Ron gave them some treats and took the coins.

9 That evening they watched a film about a bank robber.

10 Two days later they went to a museum.

11 The weather was very bad and they didn't have an umbrella.

12 They saw lots of old Roman coins.

13 They were the same as the coins Gillie found.

14 There was a man in a uniform in the museum. Gillie told him about her coins.

15 Ron ran away and the man called the police.

16 The man ate a big sandwich.

17 Two days later the police found Ron and took the coins off him.

18 Now the coins are in the museum with a sign. It says "Coins found by Gillie Woodhouse."

9 Read the story. Then put the pictures in order.

One day I went geo-caching with two of my friends, Charlie and Sue. I didn't know what geo-caching was, but Sue told me everything. I liked the idea. What a good plan for a hot Sunday morning!

We met at Sue's house. We turned on Sue's GPS and put in the coordinates. A little red sign on the GPS showed us the way to go and we started walking. We walked down the road and out of the town. We walked through some fields and we then walked up and down two hills. We were tired, hot and hungry. Nobody had any food. Should we go on? We looked down at the GPS. Only one more kilometre. We didn't want to stop now.

Fifteen minutes later, we arrived at a forest. It was large and very dark inside. Charlie was a bit scared. So was I, but I didn't say anything. Should we go in? We looked down at the GPS. Only 500 metres more. We had to go on.

Ten minutes later, we came to a river. It was quite big and there wasn't a bridge. Should we cross it? We looked down at the GPS. Only 50 metres! We all jumped into the river and swam to the opposite side.

We got out of the river. The GPS showed us that the treasure was under our feet. We looked down and saw a hole in the ground. Sue put in her hand and pulled out a box. We were all very excited. We opened the box and …

10 Write two or three sentences to complete the story in your exercise book.

SB p. 52, 53

Essential Grammar *have to – don't have to*

11 **Look at the signs and circle the correct answer.**

1 You *have to* / *don't have to* be 18 or older to get into the disco.
2 You *have to* / *don't have to* turn off your mobile phone in the cinema.
3 You *have to* / *don't have to* buy a ticket for the zoo on Sundays.
4 We *have to* / *don't have to* wear our school uniform this Friday.
5 You *have to* / *don't have to* be quiet after 10 p.m.
6 You *have to* / *don't have to* be taller than 1 metre to go on the ride.

12 **Match the rules on the hotel sign with the sentences.**

☐ You have to leave your shoes outside.
☐ You have to go to sleep at ten o'clock.
☐ You have to leave your dogs at home.
☐ You have to get up early.
☐ You have to be in the hotel by nine o'clock.
☐ You have to have cold showers.

SB p. 51, 54

…tences that are true for you.

… do a lot of homework tonight. ☐
… see my whole family this weekend. ☐
… ave to go to school tomorrow. ☐
… have to help my mum and dad in the house. ☐
… to go to the dentist's soon. ☐
6 … have to go to bed early tonight. ☐
7 I have to study for a test this week. ☐
8 I have to get up at 6 a.m. Mondays to Fridays. ☐

More Grammar *have to – don't have to*

14 Complete the sentences with the correct form of *(not) have to* and the words in the box.

invite do study take go run ~~eat~~ be

1 **A** I'm really not very hungry.
B Well, you don't have to eat everything.

2 **A** Can you help me make dinner?
B I'm sorry but I have to do my my homework.

3 **A** I think there is a problem with your laptop.
B I know. I ~~hat~~ have to take it to the shop.

4 **A** The bus leaves at 3 p.m. We've got lots of time.
B Good. So we don't have to run .

5 **A** We've got a big test tomorrow.
B Yeah. I have to study a lot tonight.

6 **A** I don't really like Colin Wood.
B Well it's your party. You don't have to invite him.

7 **A** Where's Mum?
B Her head hurts. She's in bed so you have to be quiet quiet.

8 **A** Don't forget you've got to see the doctor after school.
B But I don't feel ill any more so I don't have to go .

15 Match the sentences.

1 You don't have to cook.
2 You have to cook.
3 We don't have to run.
4 We have to run.
5 John has to study.
6 John doesn't have to study.
7 The children don't have to tidy their room.
8 The children have to tidy their room.

☐ He already knows everything on the test.
☐ The train leaves in two minutes.
☐ I did it this morning.
☐ I made dinner for you.
☐ There are toys everywhere!
☐ The test is really difficult.
☐ I'm starving*!
☐ We've got lots of time to get to the station.

VOCABULARY: *I'm starving! – Ich bin am Verhungern!

SB p. 54

16 Look at 15 again. Complete in a similar way.

1 You have to get up early. ....

....

You don't have to get up early. ....

....

2 We have to phone Vicky. ....

....

We don't have to phone Vicky. ....

....

3 Dad, you have to help me with my homework. ....

....

Dad, you don't have to help me with my homework. ....

....

4 The children have to walk to school today. ....

....

The children don't have to walk to school today. ....

....

5 The dog has to stay outside. ....

....

The dog doesn't have to stay outside. ....

....

WORD FILE

Places

SB p. 54

On holiday

MORE Words and Phrases

2	**bottom**	*It's in the bottom right-hand corner of the picture.*	untere/r/s
	left-hand	*On the left-hand side there's a lake.*	linke/r/s
	right-hand	*On the right-hand side there's a waterfall.*	rechte/r/s
3	**area**	*The picnic area was large.*	Gebiet; Region; Platz
	build	*Let's build a bridge.*	bauen
	wait a minute	*Wait a minute, I think I'll join you.*	warte mal; einen Moment
5	**move**	*We moved to Munich.*	hier: umziehen
7	**after all**	*Franz speaks good English – after all, he lives in London.*	schließlich
	bottle	*I take a bottle of water in my bag.*	Flasche
	coin	*I have several coins.*	Münze, Geldstück
	especially	*I'm always tired, especially in the morning.*	besonders
	exactly	*That's exactly right.*	genau
	find out	*Let's find out what's under this rock!*	herausfinden
	for example	*Have you got a pet? A dog, for example?*	zum Beispiel
	go along	*I went along too.*	mitgehen
	joke	*That's a joke – these coins are plastic!*	Witz
	list	*Please make a list.*	Liste
	no wonder	*He was very tired. No wonder he lost the match.*	kein Wunder
	not … any more	*We couldn't find the ring any more.*	nicht mehr
	note	*Write me a note, please.*	Notiz
	point (at)	*Please point at what you like.*	zeigen (auf)
	several	*There are several cars in the car park.*	einige, mehrere
	snack	*I'm hungry. Let's have a snack.*	Snack, Jause
	so-called	*The treasure is a small box, the so-called "cache".*	sogenannt
	something else	*There's something else in here!*	noch etwas
	unit	*You need a GPS unit.*	Gerät; Einheit
11	**imagine**	*Try to imagine how the story ends.*	sich vorstellen

UNIT 8 We might go out

Essential Vocabulary

1 Look at the pictures and complete the sentences with the words in the box.

doing
playing
staying
watching
having
tidying
doing
doing

1 Peter is .... a film.

2 Bob is .... the shopping.

3 Sue is .... her room.

4 Mike is .... volleyball.

5 Steve is .... his homework.

6 Abi is .... at a friend's house.

7 Jane is .... a party.

8 Ron is .... nothing.

More Vocabulary

2 How many words can you write with each verb?

watch
a DVD, ...
....

play
volleyball, ...
....

tidy
your room, ...
....

have
a party, ...
....

do
nothing, ...
....

stay at
a friend's house, ...
....

SB p. 56

More Grammar *going to* (negative)

11 **Complete the sentences with *not going to* and the verb from the question.**

1 **A** Are you going to invite Ben to your party?
B Yes, but I'm not going to invite .... his brother.

2 **A** Are you going to do your English homework tonight, Stephanie?
B Yes, but .... all of it.

3 **A** Is he going to tidy his room?
B Yes, but .... the living room.

4 **A** Is she going to tell her mum?
B Yes, but .... her dad.

5 **A** Are we going to have chicken for lunch?
B Yes, but .... it with chips.

12 **Write down your plans.**

Two things you're (not) going to do tonight:
- ....
- ....

Two things you're (not) going to do this weekend:
- ....
- ....

Two things you're (not) going to do next week:
- ....
- ....

More Grammar *might – might not*

13 **Match the sentence halves.**

1 It might rain
2 My head hurts
3 I need a new shirt
4 She quite likes Adele
5 He drank a lot of coffee
6 He asked her to be his wife

☐ and she might say yes.
☐ so she might buy her new CD.
☐ so I might take an aspirin.
☐ so I might go shopping tomorrow.
☐ so she's going to take an umbrella.
☐ so he might not sleep well tonight.

14 **Complete the sentences to make them true for you.**

1 After school today, I might ....
2 For dinner tonight, I might ....
3 This Sunday, I might ....
4 On Saturday morning, I might ....
5 When I'm 18, I might ....
6 When I'm 30, I might ....

SB p. 60, 61

WORD FILE

Activities

MORE Words and Phrases

1	stay at a friend's house	*Last weekend I stayed at a friend's house.*	bei einem Freund/einer Freundin übernachten
	tidy	*I don't want to tidy my room today, but I will do it tomorrow.*	aufräumen
4	**instead**	*I'm not going out. I'm going to watch TV instead.*	stattdessen
	take it easy	*I'm very tired. I'm going to take it easy this afternoon.*	sich entspannen
7	(be) ashamed	*I made a big mistake. I'm so ashamed!*	sich schämen
	excuse	*There's no excuse for bullying.*	Ausrede
	meet up	*Can we meet up on Saturday?*	sich treffen
	not feel well	*I can't come with you. I don't feel well.*	sich unwohl fühlen
	tell a lie	*Don't tell me a lie. I know it was you!*	lügen
10	crash	*I'm sorry I crashed your bike.*	zu Bruch fahren
	driving test	*To drive a car you have to take a driving test.*	Fahrprüfung
	might	*I might go shopping tomorrow if I have time.*	könnte/st/n; vielleicht (tun/sein)
	miss	*We ran to the bus stop, but we missed the bus.*	verpassen
11	get into trouble	*I might get into trouble if I do that.*	in Schwierigkeiten geraten, Ärger bekommen
13	fancy dress	*What are you wearing for the fancy dress party?*	Verkleidung, Kostüm
G	**coat**	*Please leave your coat here.*	Mantel

SWYK Units 5–8

UNIT 9 Strange things from space!

Essential Vocabulary

1 Number the words.

- ☐ land
- ☐ spaceship
- ☐ explode
- ☐ time machine
- [3] universe
- ☐ galaxy
- ☐ astronaut
- ☐ space station
- ☐ alien
- ☐ take off
- ☐ sky
- ☐ UFO
- ☐ planet

More Vocabulary

2 Write the words from 1 on the lines. Sometimes you need to change the form.

1 You can travel to the year 333 or 2,300, for example, with this. ....

2 When a thing breaks into lots of pieces it ....

3 The person who travels into space. ....

4 When a spaceship comes back to Earth, it ....

5 When a spaceship starts to fly into space, it ....

6 It's where the astronauts work and stay for some time. ....

7 At night you sometimes can see lots of stars in it. ....

8 Earth and Mars are two of these. ....

9 A group of stars in the universe. ....

10 The astronauts travel in it. ....

11 They come from another planet. ....

12 All the stars, planets and galaxies. ....

13 A spaceship from another planet. ....

SB p. 62, 63

Reading and Writing

3 **Put the summary of *A new home* on pages 62–63 of the Student's Book into the correct order.**

[6] Jenny's father got in his car and left. Jenny started tidying up. She got a broom to sweep up the seeds. Then she put them into the dustbin.

[3] When all the spaceships were ready, the Trojans left for the planet Earth. And twenty years later they arrived there.

[1] The president of Trojan asked her people to build 20,000 spaceships, because they had to leave their planet.

[5] Her father came out of the house and saw the seeds, too. He walked on some of the seeds and they went "Crack!".

[4] On Earth, Jenny was in her garden. Suddenly she saw thousands of round yellow seeds falling from the sky.

[2] With 20,000 spaceships (each could carry 10,000 Trojans) they could all go to a safe place before the other planet hit them.

4 CHOICES

A **Read the sentences. Then put the pictures in the correct order.**

1 Most of the spaceships landed in Jenny's garden.
2 Some landed near a little lake in the woods.
3 The Trojans built a palace* near the lake.
4 One day a boy was near the lake. He wanted to find insects for his collection.
5 He saw the palace and the Trojans through his magnifying glass*.
6 The next day, reporters came from all over* the world.

A

B

C

D

E

F

VOCABULARY: ***palace** – Palast; **magnifying glass** – Lupe; **from all over** – von überall her

B 1 Complete the dialogue with the sentences in the box.

Are you going to France, too?

They're in the fridge.

Where are you going this time?

Yes, there was.

You know I love them.

VOCABULARY
***time traveller** – Zeitreisende/r;
battle – Schlacht

Time traveller's wife	Are you leaving again, dear?
Time traveller*	Yes I am, dear.
Time traveller's wife	1 ....
Time traveller	To England, 1066.
Time traveller's wife	Oh, wasn't there a big battle* in 1066?
Time traveller	2 ....
Time traveller's wife	Can you bring back a present for Jonathan? It's his birthday next week.
Time traveller	OK. Anything else?
Time traveller's wife	Yes, but not from England. 3 ....
Time traveller	Maybe. Around 1900.
Time traveller's wife	Oh, good. Bring back some cheese for the party on Sunday. And dear?
Time traveller	Yes?
Time traveller's wife	Don't forget the Sachertortes for breakfast. 4 ....
Time traveller	We don't need Sachertortes. I got three yesterday. 5 ....
Time traveller's wife	Oh. OK. Thanks. Now hurry, or you'll miss the battle in 1066!

2 Tick T (*True*) or F (*False*).

1 The time traveller is going to the year 1066. T ☐ F ☐
2 He's going there because it's his birthday next week. T ☐ F ☐
3 Then he's going to England in 1900. T ☐ F ☐
4 His wife wants some cheese for the party on Sunday. T ☐ F ☐
5 He's going to get some Sachertortes. T ☐ F ☐

5 Look at the pictures and write a story in your exercise book. Think of an interesting ending.

SB p. 62, 63, 66

Essential Grammar Past simple (revision) / Past time markers

6 **Find nine more verbs and write them in the past simple. Look in all directions. (← → ↑ ↓ ↘)**

S	C	O	M	E	T	W	H
T	P	O	F	I	N	D	C
A	L	U	S	B	M	T	I
R	S	I	T	S	A	N	T
T	D	O	R	K	L	R	A
T	N	O	Y	Z	P	R	K
U	E	E	S	U	B	O	E
N	S	S	T	O	P	H	S

came
....
....
....
....
....
....
....
....
....

7 **Write the verbs in brackets in the past simple.**

A week ago I [1] watched (watch) a science-fiction film about aliens. They [2] looked (look) like us, they had jobs like us, they had lives just like us. But they gave commands. The aliens were the bosses*, and we were servants. They [3] .... (send) messages through TV, and when people were almost sleeping in front of their TVs, the messages were always there. With the help of special glasses, you [4] .... (know) who was an alien. One day a man [5] .... (find) a pair of these glasses, and he [6] .... (start) fighting the aliens. It was an old film, but I [7] .... (like) it a lot.

VOCABULARY: ***boss** – Chef

8 **What happened to Natasha? Put the sentences in the correct order.**

☐ An hour later, the car turned into a spaceship.
☐ She liked him and after two days she fell in love with* him.
☐ Ten hours later they were in the young man's home town on THX-15.
1 A month ago, Natasha met a young man.
☐ Three days ago he invited her to his home town.
☐ Yesterday they left the city in his car.

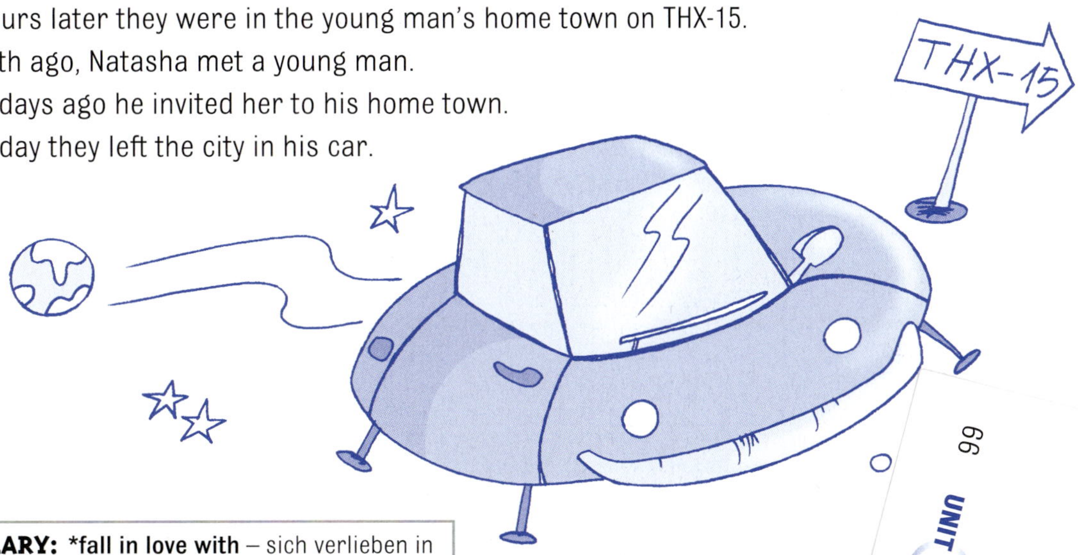

VOCABULARY: ***fall in love with** – sich verlieben in

SB p. 64

Grammar Past simple (revision) / Past time markers

Read the text and complete with the time expressions in the box.

> [illegible]xt moment
> T[illegible]e days later
> At first
> yesterday
> suddenly
> The next morning

James went into the house. He didn't see anything special in the living room, so he went upstairs to a bedroom. He looked around, and [1] .... , he saw a big book on the bed. He opened it and started to read. There were lots of stories about life on other planets. In the book he found a picture of a spaceship. James saw that there was a telephone number on the back of the book. [2] .... , James didn't know what to do. But then he picked up the phone and called the number. Somebody answered, but James didn't understand a word. James got into bed and slept all night. [3] .... , he woke up and heard a strange noise. He went to the window and looked out. There he saw the spaceship from the book. [4] .... , the door to the spaceship opened and a strange creature came out. "You called us [5] ....!" the creature said. "Come with us!" [6] .... , James was on another planet!

10 **Look at the picture story. Put the sentences in the correct order.**

- ☐ A week later, my brother was at the desk in his room again.
- ☐ Five years later, the dinosaur was as big as our house.
- ☐ He opened the box to look at the egg.
- ☐ He picked the egg up and took it to his room.
- ☐ He put it in a box near the central heating* to keep it warm.
- 1 Five years ago, my brother found an egg behind a bush in our garden.
- ☐ Suddenly, he heard a noise, but he didn't know what it was.
- ☐ The next day, he heard the noise again.
- ☐ There was no egg any more, but a little dinosaur.

VOCABULARY: ***central heating** – Zentralheizung

SB p. 66

11 Write sentences that are true for you.

1 Two weeks ago, ... (go) to school.
2 Last week, ... (hide) at home.
3 Yesterday, ... (write) a book.
4 Five hours ago, ... (not have to) listen.
5 At ten past eight this morning, ... (get) up.
6 Two hours ago, ... (not to be) at home.
7 Last night, ... (have) to sleep.
8 At midday on Sunday, ... (spend) a nice time.

Developing speaking competencies

12 Complete the dialogues.

1 **A** My rabbit died last night.
B W...................................... a p...................................... .

2 **A** Tom's ill so he can't have a party.
B T...................................... a s...................................... .

13 Complete the dialogues with your own ideas.

1 **A** ....
B What a pity.

2 **A** ....
B That's a shame.

14 Complete the dialogue with the words in the box.

pity
sit
expensive
please
a shame
sold
showing
much
ticket
row

Ben	One [1]...................................... for the 5 o'clock showing of *James Bond*, please.
Assistant	I'm sorry. It's [2]...................................... out.
Ben	That's [3]...................................... . What time is the next showing, please?
Assistant	It's not until 8 p.m.
Ben	What a [4]...................................... . That's too late.
Assistant	There's a [5]...................................... of *James Bond* at 6 p.m., but it's in 3D.
Ben	3D?
Assistant	Yes, so it's more [6]...................................... .
Ben	How [7]...................................... is it?
Assistant	It's £12.
Ben	That's OK. I'll have one ticket, [8]...................................... .
Assistant	Where would you like to [9]...................................... ?
Ben	[10]...................................... 10, please.

SB p. 66, 68

WORD FILE

To the stars

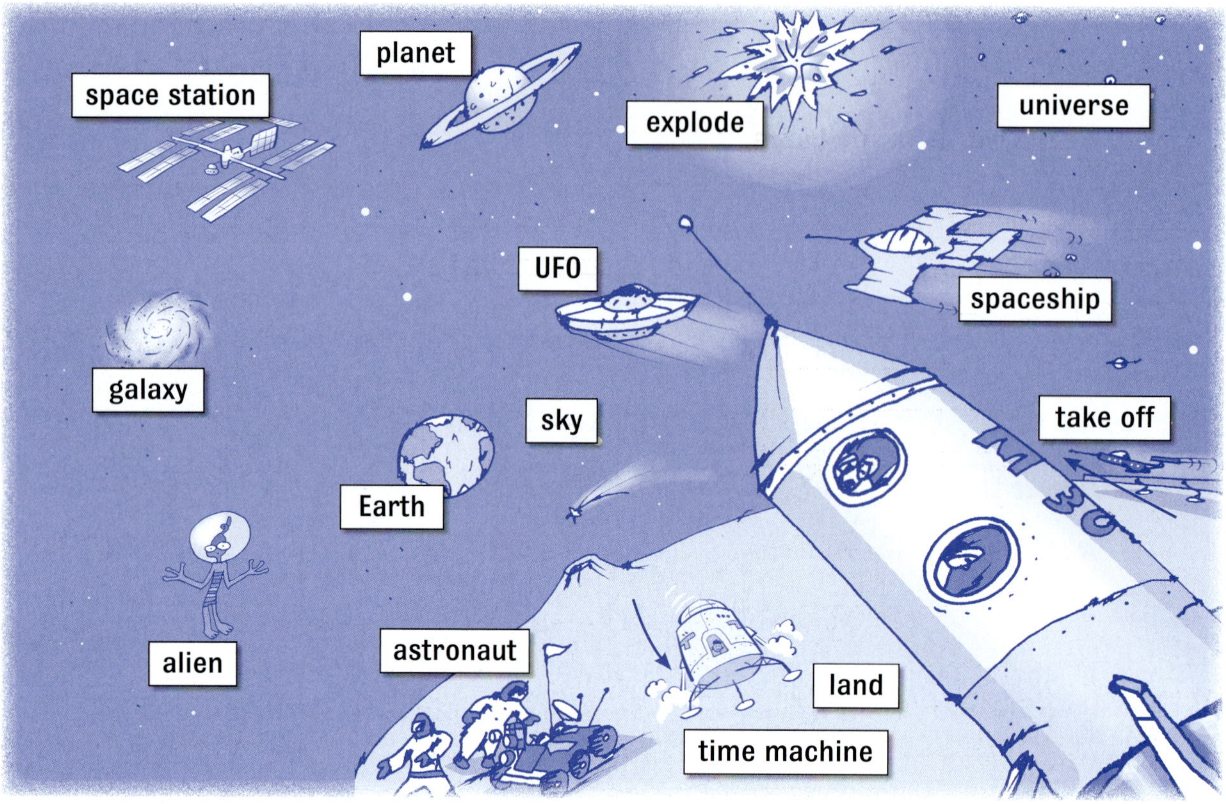

MORE Words and Phrases

1	bark	*The dog barked at the tree.*	bellen
	broom	*Use a broom to clean up the mess.*	Besen
	dustbin	*Put all the rubbish in the dustbin.*	Mülleimer
	huge	*His spaceship is huge.*	riesig, riesengroß
	take (time)	*It took them a long time to build the spaceships.*	(Zeit) brauchen
	journey	*They went on a long journey to visit their cousins.*	Reise
	one by one	*One by one, the spaceships took off.*	einer nach dem anderen
	seed	*The seeds are yellow.*	Samen
	sweep	*Please sweep the floor with this broom.*	kehren
6	**light**	*There was a green light in a window.*	Licht
8	**space**	*There are lots of stars and planets out there in space.*	Weltall
9	fake	*That picture is not real. It's a fake.*	Fälschung
	even	*My costume was so good even my mum didn't know me.*	sogar
	hoax	*The news isn't true. It's a hoax.*	Streich; Täuschung
	investigation	*The police started their investigation yesterday.*	Untersuchung, Ermittlung
	photograph	*My grandma showed me some old photographs.*	Foto(grafie)
	scientist	*Albert Einstein was a very famous scientist.*	Wissenschaftler/in
10	**absolutely**	*Are you absolutely sure? Yes, I am.*	absolut
	destroy	*In the film the aliens try to destroy Earth.*	vernichten
	look like	*John looks exactly like his father.*	aussehen wie
	take over	*The aliens wanted to take over the whole world.*	die Führung übernehmen, erobern
11	button	*If you push this button, the machine comes on.*	Knopf
	comfortable	*This chair is very comfortable.*	bequem
DVD	react	*Ms Black did not react.*	reagieren
	What a shame.		Wie schade.

Are you ready to order?

Essential Vocabulary

1 **Write the words in the boxes.**

pear
plum
peach
mushroom
olive
ham
sausage
onions
turkey
fish
cabbage
grapes
strawberry
mineral water

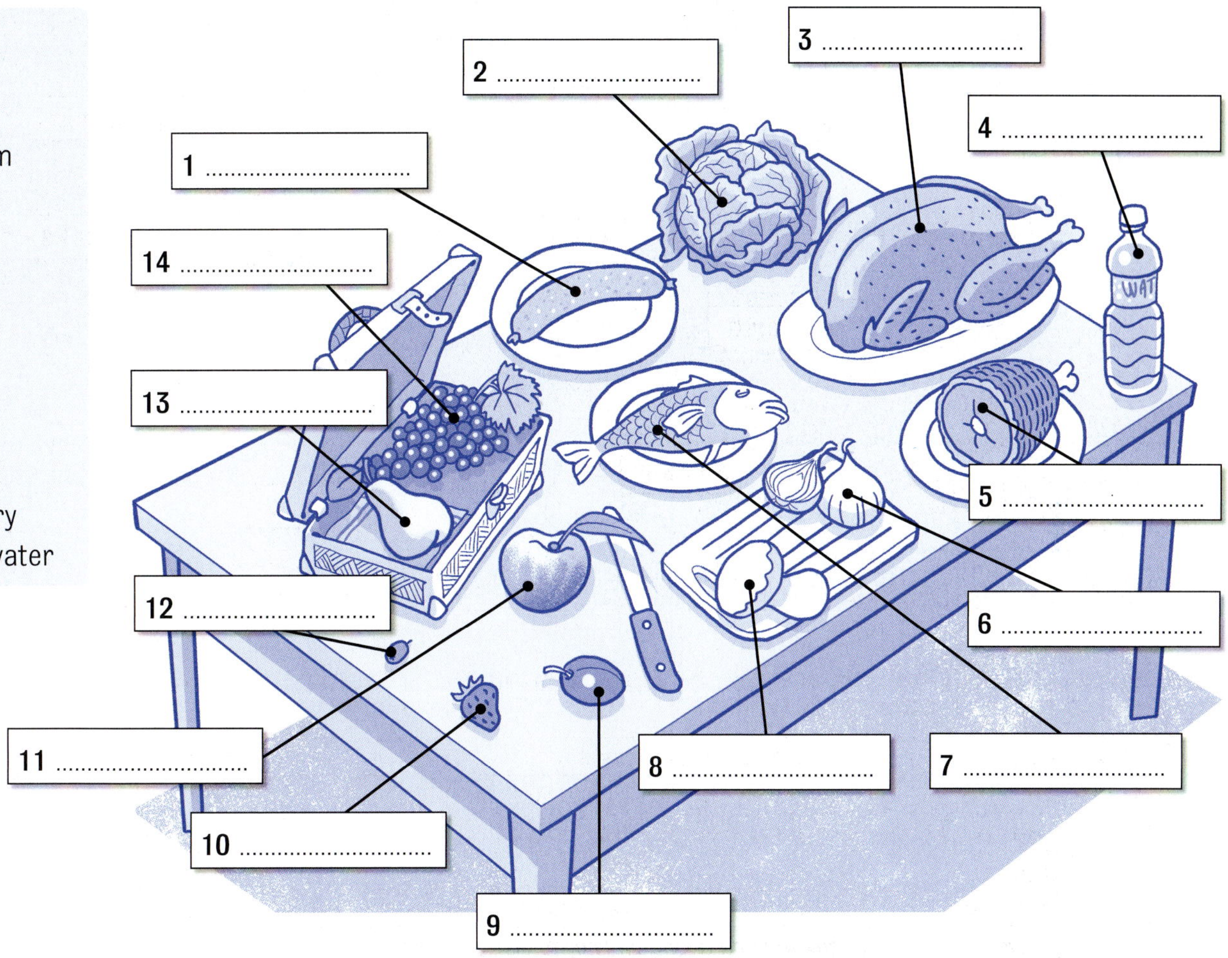

2 **Match the words with the picture. Draw lines.**

menu
waitress
waiter

order
bowl
chef
recipe

More Vocabulary

3 **Do the crossword.**

DOWN:

ACROSS:

4 **Read the menu and write the names of the pizzas under the pictures.**

Pisa
peas, onions, red peppers, cheese

Turin
egg, broccoli, onions, red peppers, cheese

Rome
sausage, tomatoes, onions, broccoli, cheese

Naples
egg, tomatoes, broccoli, peas, red peppers, cheese

Florence
tomatoes, cheese

Milan
sausage, peas, tomatoes, cheese

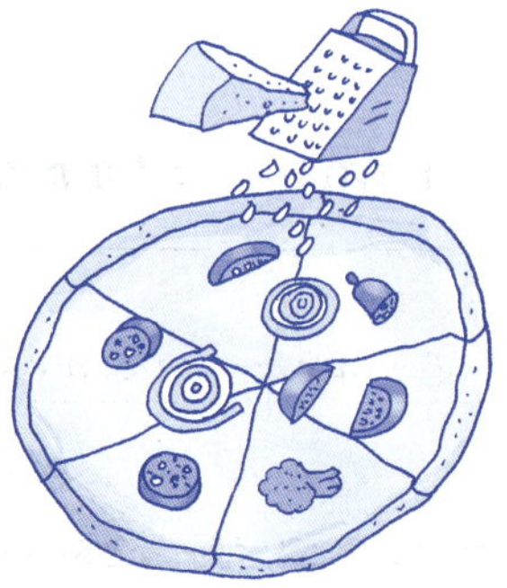

1 ....

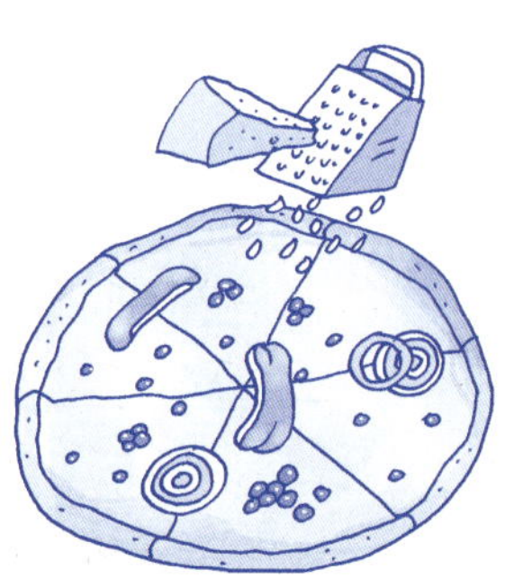

2 ....

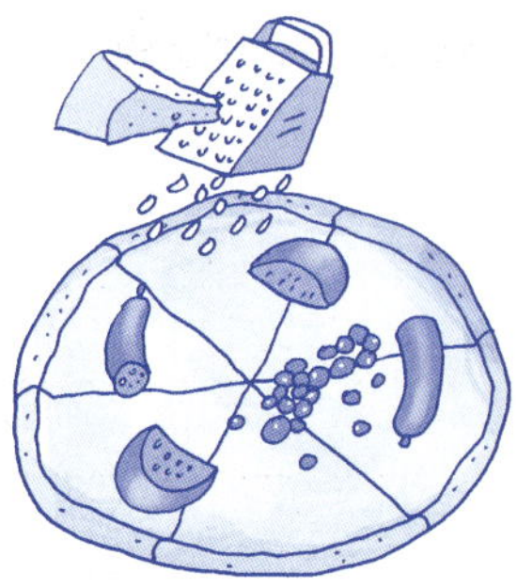

3 ....

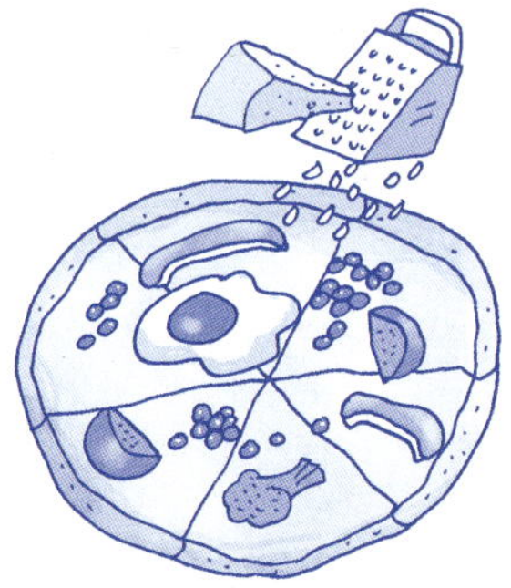

4 ....

SB p. 70, 71

Reading and Writing

5 CHOICES

A Put the dialogue in the correct order.

☐ **Waiter** OK. No onions. Would you like olives maybe?
1 **Waiter** Are you ready to order?
☐ **Waiter** Thank you. I'll bring the water straightaway.
☐ **Waiter** OK. The Rome pizza, no onions, and a mineral water.
☐ **Waiter** OK – no olives and no onions. And what would you like to drink?
☐ **Customer** No, thanks. I don't like olives.
☐ **Customer** That's right.
☐ **Customer** Yes. I'd like the Rome pizza, please. But I don't want any onions.
☐ **Customer** Water, please. A bottle of mineral water.

B Write the waiter's questions to complete the dialogue.

Waiter 1 ....
Customer Yes. I'd like the Milan pizza, please. But I don't want any peas.
Waiter 2 ....
Customer No, thanks. I don't like peppers.
Waiter OK – no peppers. 3 ....
Customer A cola please.
Waiter One cola, coming straightaway. 4 ....
Customer Not now, but I might order an ice cream later.
Waiter No problem.

6 Write a dialogue between a waiter and a customer in your exercise book.

The customer wants ...
the Turin pizza, but with no egg — an orange juice — some chocolate cake

7 Look at the picture of the sketch *The best restaurant in town*. Can you find four mistakes? The first one is done for you. Write down the other three and then look at pages 72–73 of the Student's Book to check.

They didn't drink wine*.
....
....
....
....
....

VOCABULARY: *wine – Wein

SB p. 71, 72, 73

8 Read the summary of *The best restaurant in town* and write the numbers of the missing sentences in the boxes.

A man and a woman went to a restaurant – the best restaurant in town, in fact. [3] The man and his wife ordered some onion soup for a starter. The waiter went into the kitchen. "We haven't got any onion soup," the chef said. "Run over to Johnny's Restaurant and get me some of their onion soup," the chef said to the waitress.
Johnny's Restaurant hadn't got any onion soup so the waitress brought back two bowls of tomato soup. [ ]
The man ordered beef, chips and carrots for his main course. [ ] Back in the kitchen it was the same problem – no beef and no lamb. The waitress ran to Johnny's and brought back two plates* of chicken. The man and woman were a bit angry. [ ]
But they tasted* the chicken and they were happy again. It was excellent.
The waiter asked the waitress to run over to Johnny's and get some rice pudding and chocolate ice cream. [ ] For dessert the man and the woman ordered rice pudding and chocolate ice cream.
The man and the woman loved the dessert. "This restaurant is a bit strange, but the food is great," said the man. "I think it really is the best restaurant in town."
"I'm not so sure," said his wife. "I think the best restaurant in town might be Johnny's."
[ ] The woman pointed to his ice cream. There was a little flag on the top. It said "Johnny's Restaurant."

1 "Why do you think that?" asked her husband.
2 The man and woman were surprised, but they enjoyed the soup anyway.
3 The waiter took their coats and showed them to a table next to a window.
4 They wanted beef and lamb.
5 His wife ordered lamb, potatoes and cabbage.
6 The waitress went back to Johnny's again.

VOCABULARY
***plate** – Teller; **taste** – kosten

9 Look at the pictures. Write the story *The worst restaurant in town* in your exercise book. Use the words in the box to help you.

went
dirty
waiter
knife
fly
cola
left
tasted

SB p. 72, 73, 74

Essential Grammar *some – any*

10 **Look at the picture and read the sentences. Tick T (*True*) or F (*False*).**

On the table ...

1 there is some cheesecake. T ☐ F ☐
2 there isn't any ice cream. T ☐ F ☐
3 there is some rice pudding. T ☐ F ☐
4 there is some chocolate. T ☐ F ☐

In the fruit bowl ...

5 there are some pears. T ☐ F ☐
6 there aren't any grapes. T ☐ F ☐
7 there are some strawberries. T ☐ F ☐
8 there aren't any peaches. T ☐ F ☐

On the plate ...

9 there are some peas. T ☐ F ☐
10 there is some chicken. T ☐ F ☐
11 there aren't any potatoes. T ☐ F ☐
12 there isn't any beef. T ☐ F ☐

11 **Circle the correct option.**

1 They haven't got *some* / *any* children.
2 Can I have *some* / *any* ice cream, please?
3 There are *some* / *any* books on my desk.
4 She hasn't got *some* / *any* friends.
5 I've got *some* / *any* money. Here you are.
6 I don't want *some* / *any* soup, thanks.

12 **Match the questions and answers.**

1 Would you like some orange juice?
2 Do you want some chocolate?
3 Can you give me some money?
4 Have you got any children?
5 Does your head hurt?
6 Is there any ice cream in the freezer?

☐ No, but I'm going to buy some at the supermarket.
☐ Yes. Have you got any aspirin?
☐ Yes. Two sons and a daughter.
☐ Yes, please, I'm very thirsty.
☐ I'm sorry. I haven't got any.
☐ No, thanks. I don't like sweets.

SB p. 75

More Grammar *some – any*

13 **Look at the picture and complete the sentences. Use *some* or *any*.**

In the fruit bowl …

there are some .... apples.

.... grapes.

.... plums.

.... strawberries.

.... oranges.

.... peaches.

14 **Complete the dialogue with *some* or *any*.**

Dad Have [1]........................ fruit for dessert.

Jenny I don't want [2]........................ fruit. Haven't we got [3]........................ ice cream?

Dad Yes, there's [4]........................ ice cream in the freezer, but …

Jenny Well, can I have [5]........................ ?

Dad No, you can't. You can have [6]........................ fruit.

Jenny But I don't like fruit.

Dad Don't be silly. Here, have [7]........................ strawberries.

Jenny Can I have [8]........................ strawberry ice cream?

Dad No!

15 **Look in the fridge for thirty seconds and remember as much as you can. Then cover the picture and write sentences.**

1 pears
There are some pears.

2 strawberries
There aren't any strawberries.

3 onions
....

4 grapes
....

5 peppers
....

6 tomatoes
....

7 cabbage
....

8 lamb
....

9 chicken
....

10 chocolate
....

11 cheesecake
....

12 cheese
....

SB p. 75

WORD FILE

Food and drink

In a restaurant

MORE Words and Phrases

1	pancakes	*I love making pancakes.*	Palatschinken, Pfannkuchen
	pie	*Chicken pie is my favourite meal.*	Pastete; Kuchen
3	**basket**	*There are tomatoes in the shopping basket.*	Korb
	slice	*Two big slices of pizza for me, please!*	Stück
7	**main course**	*We had chicken and chips for our main course.*	Hauptgang
	starter	*They had tomato soup as a starter.*	Vorspeise
	straightaway	*You're hungry? I'll bring the soup straightaway!*	sofort
8	couple	*The couple sat together in the restaurant.*	Paar
10	**serve**	*The waitress served them coffee after the dessert.*	servieren
	stew	*We had Irish stew for lunch.*	Eintopf
DVD	**by the way**	*By the way, I'm Emma.*	übrigens
	It's no trouble at all.		Es ist überhaupt kein Problem.

Reading and Writing

6 Match the sentence halves.

1 We know about life in ancient Egypt
2 People in ancient Egypt wore light clothes
3 People wore sandals or
4 The sandals were made
5 Men and women cared about their looks and
6 Many Egyptians worked as farmers, but
7 Weavers made beautiful clothes and people
8 People ate fish, meat, fruit
9 Hunting and fishing were the most
10 Children played ball games

☐ went barefoot.
☐ they also had to help build the pyramids.
☐ paid for them with salt, food and other things.
☐ from objects found in tombs.
☐ and a lot of vegetables.
☐ because it was very hot.
☐ popular sports for the men.
☐ wore make-up and jewellery.
☐ and had little animals made from wood.
☐ of palm leaves.

7 Put the dialogue in the correct order.

☐ **A** How long did it take?
☐ **A** That's a lot of stones!
☐ **A** How heavy?
☐ **A** Wow – that's high! How long is it?
☐ **A** Did you go to a pyramid when you were in Egypt?
☐ **B** More than 230 metres. And they needed a hundred thousand men to build it.
☐ **B** About twenty years. And it was really hard work. The stones were heavy.
☐ **B** Well, each one was about two thousand kilograms! And … the pyramid has got over two million stones in it.
☐ **B** Yes, we went to the one for Pharaoh Khufu. It was amazing! You know, it's over 140 metres high.

8 Put the verbs in the box in the correct places.

believed
broke
climbed
died
found
guarded
knew
put
stole
woke

When a pharaoh 1 .... , the priests 2 .... the mummy inside a pyramid. The ancient Egyptians 3 .... that, after a long time, the pharaoh's spirit 4 .... up and 5 .... up the steps of the pyramid to meet Ra, the sun god. The people put things like food, clothes and jewellery in the pyramid with the mummy. Of course, everyone 6 .... that there were wonderful things inside the pyramid, so soldiers 7 .... the tombs day and night to stop thieves. But hundreds of years later, robbers 8 .... into the pyramids. They 9 .... the tombs and 10 .... the clothes and jewellery.

SB p. 79, 80

9 CHOICES

A Complete the text with the words in the box.

mummy	young
famous	old
find	died
found	clothes
became	

One of the most [1] .... pharaohs was Tutankhamun. He [2] .... pharaoh when he was very [3] .... Tutankhamun [4] .... when he was only nineteen years [5] .... The robbers didn't [6] .... his tomb. When an Englishman called Howard Carter [7] .... the tomb, it was still full of wonderful [8] .... and jewellery. He also found the [9] .... of Tutankhamun.

B Read the summary of the story in the Student's Book on page 82. There is a mistake in each sentence. Cross it out and write the correct word.

The curse of the pharaoh

1 Hannah, Luke and their parents went to visit a pyramid with a ~~friend~~. guide..................

2 The guide told them about a group of tourists who tried to find a tomb in the pyramid, but never came back. ....

3 He said: "The story of the pharaoh killed them!" ....

4 Hannah laughed and shouted something to Luke, but Luke didn't hear her. ....

5 "Look!" he said. "There's a hole in the floor!" ....

6 They climbed through the hole, and suddenly there was a loud wind, and a stone closed the hole. ....

7 The children tried to break the stone, but they couldn't – they couldn't get out again. ....

8 So they walked along a corridor in the dark until they saw an open window and looked out. ....

9 They saw men building another pyramid. The men talked like people from ancient Egypt! ....

10 Write the story in your exercise book. Make up your own ending.

The pharaoh died and the people were very unhappy. ...

SB p. 80, 81, 82

Essential Grammar Irregular plurals

11 **Write one word in each box.**

Singular	Plural
man	men
woman	
	children
person	
foot	

Singular	Plural
	teeth
fish	
knife	
	thieves
sheep	

12 **Use words from 11 to complete the conversations.**

1 **A** Are there any forks* in the drawer?
B Er – no, only spoons* and ....

2 **A** Can I wear your shoes?
B Don't be silly – my .... are smaller than yours.

3 **A** Did you catch anything in the river today?
B Yes, we caught ten really nice ....

4 **A** My older sister is twenty-two and she has a husband.
B Has she got any .... ?

5 **A** I can't go to sleep!
B Why don't you count .... ?

VOCABULARY
***fork** – Gabel; **spoon** – Löffel

13 **Look at the picture for a minute. Then cover and complete the sentences.**

In the picture there are …

1 eight children ....
2 five ....
3 three ....
4 seven ....
5 four ....
6 nine ....

SB p. 79, 83

Essential Grammar Questions with *"Who … ?"*

14 **Match the questions and pictures.**

1 Who found the mummy?
2 Who wrote this email?
3 Who gave him the present?
4 Who went with you to Egypt?
5 Who broke the vase?

More Grammar Questions with *"Who … ?"*

15 **Write the questions.**

1 Someone phoned me last night!
Who phoned you ……………………………… ?

2 Someone gave Sally a present yesterday.
……………………………… ?

3 Someone ate all the chocolate!
……………………………… ?

4 There are six girls in the class – one of them loves Billy!
……………………………… ?

5 I've got a lot of friends – one of them lives in that house.
……………………………… ?

6 One boy forgot his homework.
……………………………… ?

7 Someone told you my secret.
……………………………… ?

8 One girl lost her schoolbag.
……………………………… ?

16 **Do the quiz. Match the questions and answers. Do you know who the people in the pictures are? Discuss with a partner.**

1 Who discovered America?
2 Who plays Harry Potter in the films?
3 Who painted the *Mona Lisa*?
4 Who sings "Born this way"?
5 Who wrote *Romeo and Juliet*?
6 Who invented the telephone?
7 Who found Tutankhamun's tomb?
8 Who wrote *Harry Potter*?

☐ Leonardo da Vinci.
☐ Christopher Columbus.
☐ Lady Gaga.
☐ J.K. Rowling.
☐ Alexander Graham Bell.
☐ Howard Carter.
☐ William Shakespeare.
☐ Daniel Radcliffe.

SB p. 80, 83

WORD FILE

In ancient Egypt

On a farm

Jobs

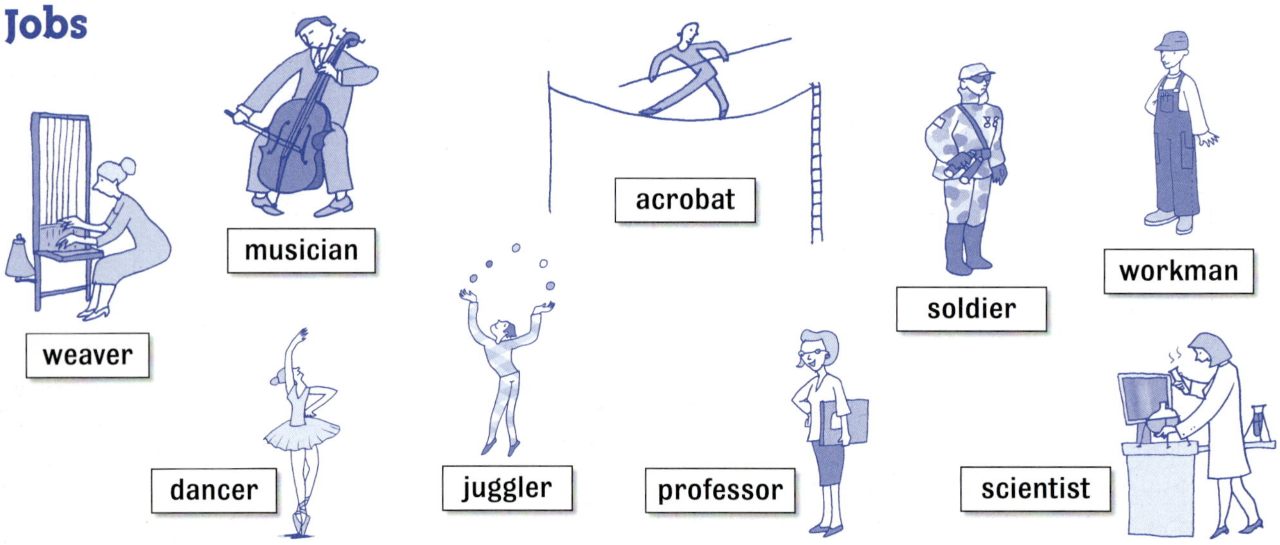

MORE Words and Phrases

1	ancient	*The ancient Egyptians lived along the River Nile.*	(ur-)alt
2	**actually**	*Actually his name isn't Peter – it's Brian!*	eigentlich
	bath	*When it is hot I have a bath every day.*	Bad
	cross	*On top of a mountain there is usually a cross.*	Kreuz
	goose (pl geese)	*The farmer has lots of geese on his farm.*	Gans
	human	*The human body has two arms and two legs.*	Mensch; menschlich
	invent	*Alexander Bell invented the telephone.*	erfinden
	mostly	*She goes to see her grandparents every week, mostly on Thursdays.*	meistens
	per cent (%)	*90 per cent of Egyptians live near the Nile.*	Prozent (%)
	plant	*Because of the River Nile, plants grow well in Egypt.*	Pflanze
	probably	*Eye glasses probably came from Italy.*	vermutlich
	religion	*Buddhism and Islam are important religions in Asia.*	Religion
	tricky	*This question is tricky because there are actually two correct answers.*	betrügerisch; hier: schwierig, kompliziert
3	**care about**	*Egyptians cared a lot about their looks.*	Wert legen auf
	fat	*I didn't like the meat. There was a lot of fat in it.*	Fett
	jewellery	*She spends lots of money on jewellery.*	Schmuck
	leaf (pl leaves)	*The leaves on the tree were all yellow and brown.*	Blatt
	light	*Wear something light today. It's very hot.*	leicht
	looks	*Sally has everything – good looks and lots of money!*	Aussehen
	made of ...	*Egyptian sandals were made of palm leaves.*	aus ... gemacht
	melt	*The ice cream melted in the hot sun.*	schmelzen
	pay (for)	*They paid for the food and then left the restaurant.*	bezahlen
	sell	*They sell a lot of different perfumes at the chemist's.*	verkaufen
	smell	*Mmm, that pizza smells good!*	riechen
	worker	*Many workers helped to build the pyramids.*	Arbeiter/in
7	**indeed**	*Is that Petra over there at the bus stop? Yes, indeed it is.*	tatsächlich
8	**born**	*He was born in England.*	geboren
	cheek	*His cheeks were red in the cold air.*	Wange
	discover	*Howard Carter discovered the tomb in 1922.*	entdecken
	Englishman	*An Englishman found Tutankhamun's tomb.*	Engländer
	full of	*The pyramid was full of wonderful clothes and jewellery.*	voll von
	guard	*The "curse of the pharaoh" helped guard the treasure.*	bewachen
	interested in	*She is very interested in animals.*	interessiert an
	spirit	*The pharaoh was dead, but people believed his spirit lived on.*	Geist
	step	*You must climb up the steps to get a good view.*	Stufe
	wound	*There was the same wound on the pharaoh's cheek.*	Wunde
9	**choose**	*Did you choose strawberry or apricot jam?*	auswählen
	jam	*I like stawberry jam on toast for breakfast.*	Marmelade
10	**centre**	*The shops are all in the city centre.*	Zentrum; Mitte
	fill	*Fill the pot with water.*	füllen
	group	*I went on holiday with a group of friends last year.*	Gruppe
	second	*Wait a second! I forgot my bag.*	Sekunde
	torch	*To explore tombs, you must use a torch.*	Taschenlampe
11	corridor	*There was a light at the end of the corridor.*	Gang
	fall over	*The little girl fell over and cut her knee.*	hinfallen; umfallen
	shocked	*She was shocked when she saw the accident.*	schockiert
	voice	*Suddenly they heard voices.*	Stimme
	wide	*There's a very wide road in front of our house.*	weit; breit

UNIT 12 Families

Essential Vocabulary

1 Write the words in the family tree.

grandfather
grandmother
father
mother
aunt
uncle
cousin
son
daughter

2 Write the words.

1 gle / sin / rent / pa
single parent
2 rents / grand / pa
....
3 ns / twi
....
4 sin / cou
....
5 ter / daugh
....
6 nt / au
....
7 dren / chil
....
8 ied / marr
....
9 bies / ba
....

3 Write the words from 2 under the pictures.

1 cousin

2 ....

3 ....

4 ....

5 ....

6 ....

7 ....

8 ....

9 ....

SB p. 85, 87

More Vocabulary

4 **Find the thirteen family words. (← → ↑ ↓ ↘ ↙)**

N	E	R	D	L	I	H	C	D	G	A	N	R
N	L	E	A	I	R	E	T	H	G	U	A	D
I	E	H	R	U	J	N	A	S	O	B	E	S
S	P	T	L	A	N	D	M	T	I	R	I	O
U	S	A	R	E	H	T	O	M	Q	S	K	N
O	T	F	R	A	W	B	R	O	T	H	E	R
C	I	Y	L	I	M	A	F	E	Y	U	W	N
G	R	A	N	D	P	A	R	E	N	T	S	A
W	T	S	X	E	L	C	N	U	H	S	A	T

....
....
....
....
....
....
....
....
....
....
....
....

Reading and Writing

5 **Read the text in the Student's Book on page 85 about Angelina Jolie and her family again. Then tick the correct box.**

1 Angelina Jolie gives a lot of money to help
☐ refugees. ☐ farmers. ☐ film stars.

2 In 2005, Angelina Jolie adopted a child from
☐ Asia. ☐ Africa. ☐ South America.

3 Brad Pitt was her
☐ second husband. ☐ first husband. ☐ third husband.

4 Her first child, Shiloh Nouvel, was born in
☐ 2004. ☐ 2005. ☐ 2006.

5 Angelina Jolie adopted
☐ two children. ☐ six children. ☐ three children.

6 Angelina Jolie adopted … from Asia.
☐ one child. ☐ two children. ☐ three children.

6 **Work out how old the following people are.**

Mr King is nine times as old as* his granddaughter Hanna.
His son John is three years older than his daughter Susan.
Susan is half as old as Mrs King.
Together John's children, the twins, are as old as their aunt Susan.
Susan's daughter Hanna is 8. She's half as old as the twins.

Mr King: ....
Mrs King: ....
John King: ....
Susan King: ....
The twins: ....
Hanna: ..8..

VOCABULARY: *nine times as old as – neun Mal so alt wie

SB p. 85, 87

7 CHOICES

A **Complete Sam's text with words from the box.**

raining
played
England
juggle
easy
was
do
go out
difficult

Last summer I met a girl from 1 ....
Her name was Annabel. She 2 ....
very nice. One day it was 3 .... and
we couldn't 4 ....
We 5 .... some games. Then Annabel
showed me how to juggle tennis balls. I loved that, but
it looked very 6 .... "I cannot do this,"
I thought. "It's not 7 .... !"
But then Annabel helped me, and now I can
8 .... It's the coolest thing
I can 9 ....

B **Read the texts on page 86 of your Student's Book again. Then write a text (60–80 words) about yourself.**

Write about:

- the coolest thing you can do
- when you learnt it
- how you learnt it
- the person that showed you how to do it

Essential Grammar *like (doing)*

8 **What do they like? Write sentences.**

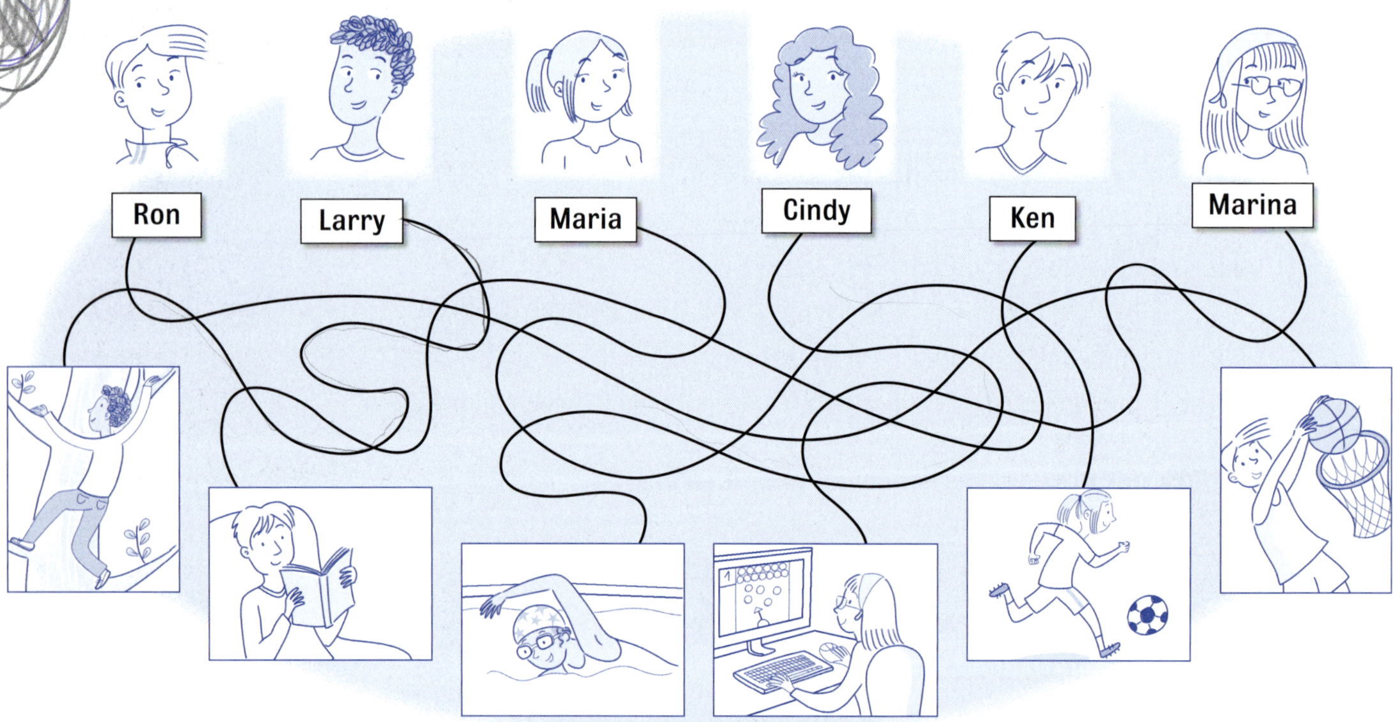

1 Ron likes playing basketball.
2 Larry likes climbing trees
3 Maria likes playing football
4 Cindy likes swimming
5 Ken likes reading
6 Marina likes playing video-games

SB p. 86

Essential Grammar *must – mustn't*

9 **Write *must* or *mustn't*.**

1 You mustn't feed the animals.
2 You must turn right at the crossing.
3 You must stop for sheep crossing.
4 You mustn't swim here.
5 You mustn't leave your boots here.
6 You mustn't run in the corridors.

More Grammar *like (doing)*

10 **Write sentences about the people below.**

1 Christopher likes dancing, but he doesn't like singing.

2 Harry likes skateboarding, but he doesn't like roller-skating.

3 Ada likes reading, but she doesn't like drawing.

4 Tanya likes cooking, but she doesn't like doing the washing up.

5 Joe likes juggling, but he doesn't like dancing.

6 My grandpa likes watching TV, but he doesn't like going to the cinema

SB p. 88, 89

11 Complete the sentences so they are true for you.

1 (basketball) I don't like playing basketball. / I like playing basketball.

2 (reading) I don't like reading / I like reading

3 (swimming) I don't like swimming / I like swimming

4 (playing computer games) I don't like playing computer games / I like

5 (climbing trees) I don't like climbing trees / I like climbing trees

6 (playing football) I don't like playing football / I like playing football

12 Complete the text.

When I was a kid, I liked all kinds of sports. I liked [1] football ,

I liked [2] swimming , and I even liked

[3] climbing .

Today I'm a bit lazy. I don't like [4] getting up  in the morning,

I don't like [5] running  or [6] driving a bike .

What do I like? I like [7] watching TV  television,

[8] eating  and [9] sleaping !

13 Write sentences about when you were younger.

1 (sport) When I was a kid, I didn't like playing football, but now I love it.
When I was a kid, I liked playing football, but now I like playing tennis.

2 (TV programmes) ....

3 (books, magazines, etc.) ....

4 (school subjects) ....

5 (food) ....

6 (free time activity) ....

SB p. 86, 89

More Grammar *must – mustn't*

14 **Complete the dialogue with the sentences in the box.**

Is there anything I can do?

10 o'clock as usual.

or you'll feel bad all night.

You must be home by 10 o'clock.

Jo OK, Mum, I'm off to the youth club.

Mum Wait, Jo. 1 ~~You must~~ You must be home by 10 o'clock

Jo I know, Mum. 2 10 o'clock as usual

Mum And you mustn't eat and drink too much, 3 or you fell bad all night

Jo I know, Mum. I never eat too much.

Mum But you drink too much cola, I know you. You mustn't, OK?

Jo OK. 4 Is there anything I can do

Mum Sure. You must have fun.

Jo Ha, ha. Is that an order?

15 **Write six rules about your school. Say what students *must* / *mustn't* do.**

16 **My aunty Mary doesn't like children. Write down the things you *mustn't* do in her house. Use the words in the box to help you.**

run down the stairs
use
listen
take
put

1 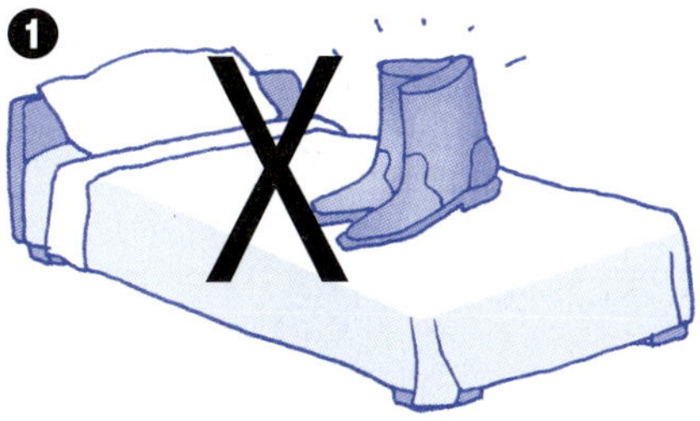

2 

3 

4 

5 

1 You mustn't put your boots on your bed.
2 You mustn't listen to music
3 You mustn't run down the stairs.
4 You mustn't use the phone
5 You mustn't take food from the freezer

Developing speaking competencies

17 **Put the dialogue in order.**

☐	**Assistant**	And would you like anything to drink?
1	**Assistant**	Good evening. Can I take your order?
☐	**Assistant**	A cheese and tomato pizza?
☐	**Assistant**	OK. That's one apple juice.
☐	**Assistant**	An orange juice. And is that eat in or take away?
☐	**Assistant**	OK. That's £12, please.
☐	**Benjamin**	Hang on. No, I think I'll have a ham and mushroom one.
☐	**Benjamin**	Take away, please.
☐	**Benjamin**	An apple juice, please.
☐	**Benjamin**	Yes, I'd like a cheese and tomato pizza, please.
☐	**Benjamin**	No, wait a second. I'll have an orange juice.

WORD FILE

In a family

SB p. 90

MORE Words and Phrases

3	**all over**	*She's famous all over the world.*	überall
	adopt	*They adopted three children.*	adoptieren
	daughter	*Her daughter's name is Shiloh Nouvel.*	Tochter
	seven-month-old	*Maddox was a seven-month-old baby.*	sieben Monate alt
	three-year-old	*Pax Thien was a three-year-old boy from Vietnam.*	dreijährig
5	**breathe**	*I like to breathe the clean air in the mountains.*	atmen
	burn	*You can burn wood on a fire.*	(ver-)brennen
	chance	*I had the chance to go to Australia on holiday.*	Chance
	couldn't	*I'm sorry but I couldn't find your mobile phone anywhere.*	konnte/n nicht, konntest nicht
	countryside	*They like going to the countryside on holiday.*	Land(schaft)
	course	*We went on a course to learn French.*	Kurs
	during	*They met up three times during the week for lunch.*	während
	farmer	*He helped a farmer to drive a tractor.*	Bauer, Bäuerin
	foreign language	*She speaks three foreign languages.*	Fremdsprache
	hang around	*I don't want to hang around for long. I want to go home.*	herumlungern
	miss	*I really miss all my friends.*	vermissen
	myself	*I cut myself with a knife last week.*	mich selbst
	not that difficult	*The job wasn't that difficult after all.*	nicht so schwierig
	panic	*When you get scared, try not to panic.*	in Panik geraten
	tractor	*The farmer has three big tractors on his farm.*	Traktor
	without	*I did the test this time without making a mistake!*	ohne
7	tool	*You use tools to make or build things.*	Werkzeug
9	Portuguese	*My friend Rui speaks Portuguese.*	portugiesisch; Portugiesisch
	refugee camp	*She had to leave her country and now lives in a refugee camp.*	Flüchtlingslager
	study	*My cousin studied at the university in Birmingham.*	studieren
	translate	*My uncle translates from Portuguese into English.*	übersetzen
	university	*There is no university in this town.*	Universität
	war	*We had to leave because of the war.*	Krieg
12	till	*Can I stay out till ten o'clock?*	bis
13	**borrow (from)**	*Can I borrow a ring from you?*	ausleihen (von)
	chat	*Don't chat with strangers.*	chatten
	delete	*Oops, I have deleted your file.*	löschen
	Forget it!		Vergiss es!
	print out	*I don't print out web pages.*	ausdrucken
	switch off/on	*Switch off the computer!*	aus-/einschalten
15	anecdote	*That anecdote he told us was very funny.*	Anekdote
	genius	*He was a mathematician and a genius.*	Genie
	mathematician	*A mathematician has to be very good at Maths!*	Mathematiker/in
	move house	*We're moving house to London next month.*	umziehen
18	**between**	*He's standing between the two trees in the park.*	zwischen
	leaflet	*Here's a leaflet with all the information you need.*	Broschüre
	owner	*Who is the owner of this hotel?*	Eigentümer/in

6 Write the numbers of the sentences in the pictures.

1 I can pass through a locked door easily.
2 Gozo likes screaming loudly.
3 Now you have to walk quietly.
4 Don't go so fast!
5 A ghost must walk through a wall very slowly.
6 She can take off her head really well.

7 CHOICES

A Match the sentence halves for a summary of the story *Abracadabra, one, two, three.*

1 Mr Blogg was Debbie and
2 He didn't like the children and
3 When Robert's football landed next to
4 When the children had a party, Mr Blogg
5 Debbie wanted to put a
6 They got five things from Mr Blogg and
7 Then they sprinkled it
8 Some time later there was
9 The policeman said, "Mr Blogg had a
10 In his car they found a lot of stolen

☐ in Mr Blogg's garden.
☐ a police car outside Mr Blogg's house.
☐ made a brown liquid*.
[1] Robert's neighbour.
☐ computers.
☐ spell on Mr Blogg.
☐ car accident."
☐ the children didn't like him.
☐ Mr Blogg's deckchair, he put a nail in it.
☐ complained about the noise.

VOCABULARY: ***liquid** – Flüssigkeit

SB p. 92–95

B **Read the summary of *Abracadabra, one, two, three* and write the** ... **complete it.**

Debbie and her brother Robert were playing football behind the house. The ball landed in the garden next door. Robert climbed

over the [1]................................  to get it. The ball was next

to the [2]................................  of their neighbour, Mr Blogg. He didn't like the children and Robert was a bit scared. Mr Blogg saw Robert and shouted. Robert jumped back over the fence. Mr Blogg threw their ball back. But

now it had a big [3]............................  in it.

The next Saturday was Debbie's birthday. She had a party in the garden with lots of friends. They made a fire in the garden and made

[4]................................  on it. Mr Blogg complained about the smoke and the noise. Three days later, their cat Snowy was ill. Debbie was sure Mr Blogg had something to do with it.

Debbie had a book on magic.

It had lots of [5]............................ in it. She wanted to put a spell on Mr Blogg. They needed five things from Mr Blogg to make the spell. That night, the children climbed into his garden. They found five things:

half a cigar, a piece o...

half a hot dog and a ...

The next morning they put a... in a pot and filled it with water. Th...

put the pot on the [7]................................  and made a brown liquid*.

Then they went back to Mr Blogg's 

garden and [8]................................ the brown liquid on the grass. Suddenly Mr Blogg arrived and shouted at them, and the children ran away quickly.

The children spent the afternoon at their grandmother's house. When they got back home, there was a police car outside the house. "What's the matter?" Robert asked the policeman.

"Mr Blogg had a car accident in town," the policeman told them. "And when

we looked in his [9]................................ we found a lot of stolen computers.

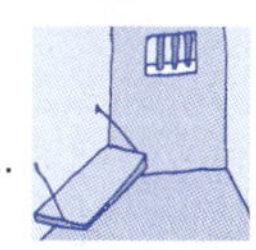

Your neighbour's in [10]............................ now." The children smiled. What a great spell!

VOCABULARY: *liquid – Flüssigkeit

8 Complete the sentences about the story *Abracadabra, one, two, three.*

1 Debbie and Robert lived next ....
2 Mr Blogg didn't like ....
3 He did lots of terrible things – for example, he put a nail ....
4 The children wanted to ....
5 They needed five ....
6 They sprinkled ....
7 Mr Blogg had a car accident and the police found ....
8 The spell worked because ....

9 Write a story called *The wrong spell* in your exercise book. Think about your answers to these questions to help you write the story.

- Who made the spell?
- What was the spell for?
- How did he or she make the spell?
- Why did it go wrong?
- What happened?

SB p. 94, 95

ntial Grammar Adverbs of manner

Write the adverbs.

adjective	adverb	adjective	adverb	adjective	adverb
loud	loudly	nervous	....	happy	....
quiet	....	careful	....	angry	....
quick	....	easy	....	fast	....
slow	....	bad	....	good	....

11 Read the sentences. Underline the adjective and circle the (adverb) in each one.

1 Dad washed his new car (carefully).
2 The children walked nervously over the dangerous bridge.
3 The pizza was delicious and Sally ate it quickly.
4 The game was difficult and United played badly.
5 The farmer shouted angrily at the naughty* children.
6 John's bike was old, but he rode it fast.

> **VOCABULARY**
> ***naughty** – ungezogen, frech

12 Complete the sentences with the adverbs of the adjectives in the box.

bad
careful
good
happy
fast
slow

1 She's running very ....

2 He's working really ....

3 It's walking .... to the other side of the street.

4 She's laughing ....

5 I did .... in the test today.

6 They're playing very ....

SB p. 96, 97

More Grammar Adverbs of manner

13 **Use the adverbs of the adjectives in brackets to complete the sentences.**

1 **A** He plays football really .... (good)
B Yes, he wants to be a star.

2 **A** I don't think the teacher was very happy.
B No, she looked at us really .... (angry)

3 **A** Sh! Talk .... (quiet)
B Why?
A Henry's trying to sleep.

4 **A** Are we in a hurry?
B No.
A So, don't walk so .... (quick)

5 **A** Slower, Dad, slower!
B Yes, you're driving too .... (fast)

6 **A** Is the climb very difficult?
B Yes, so you should go very .... (careful)

14 **Read the text and circle the correct options.**

I'm a ghost hunter! I hunt ghosts and when I catch them I take them to a castle on an island in the north of Scotland. There they can rattle their chains and make [1] *loud / loudly* noises. There they can wait [2] *quiet / quietly* for other ghosts. They can go "Boo!" and laugh [3] *happy / happily* when the other ghosts are scared. On the island they can't scare people like you and me.
I'm not scared [4] *easy / easily.* A good ghost hunter isn't scared of ghosts! But sometimes ghosts make me [5] *nervous / nervously,* because they play tricks. They hide their heads, and they go through walls [6] *quick / quickly.* And when I follow them, I hit my head. Hunting ghosts is what I do [7] *good / well.* Only I sometimes have bad dreams. I dream that a big ghost catches me and takes me to the north of Scotland. There, hundreds of [8] *angry / angrily* ghosts are waiting for me. Luckily it's only a dream.

15 **Answer the questions about yourself.**

1 What do you do well?

....

2 What do you do badly?

....

3 What do you do carefully?

....

4 What do you do easily?

....

5 What do you do quickly?

....

6 What do you do happily?

....

SB p. 97

11 Complete the dialogue with the possessive pronouns.

hers
yours
mine

Dimitri	I hate this!
Ron	Well, whose idea was it to go for a walk?
Dimitri	It certainly wasn't [1].. .
Ron	No? I thought it was [2].. .
Dimitri	Never. Check with Anna, I think it was [3].. .
Ron	I can't, she's too far ahead already.

12 Complete with the possessive pronouns in the box.

mine
theirs
ours
his
mine
theirs

Camp guide	Fred and Hannah, is this your GPS?
Fred and Hannah	Yes, it's [1].................................... .
Camp guide	And is this your cap, Tony?
Tony	No, it isn't [2].................................... . Ask Peter. I think it's [3].................................... .
Camp guide	And what about these trainers?
Maria	They're [4].................................... , sir.
Camp guide	Right, here you go, Maria. And these maps belong to the Hart twins, right?
Tony	No, they aren't [5].................................... . They're Anita's. [6].................................... are much older.

Developing speaking competencies

13 Match the pictures and the sentences.

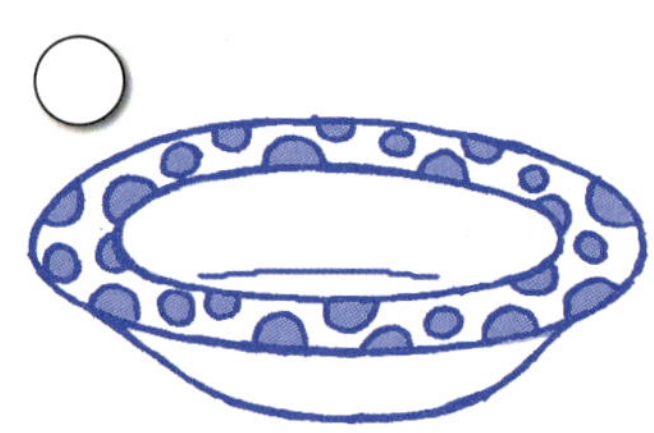

1 It's made of leather. It's plain.
2 It's made of leather. It's spotted.
3 It's made of plastic. It's striped.
4 It's made of plastic. It's spotted.
5 It's made of cotton. It's plain.
6 It's made of cotton. It's striped.

SB p. 103, 104

14 Put the words in order to make the dialogues.

A made / your / what's / of / bag / ? — A What's your bag made of?
B made / it's / leather / of — B ....
A sure / you / are / ? — A ....
B am / yes / I / was / it / expensive / really — B ....

C tie / your / what's / like / ? — C ....
D blue / it's / white / spots / with — D ....
C certain / are / you / ? — C ....
D not / no / I'm / with / spots / it's / white / blue — D ....

WORD FILE

Inside a room

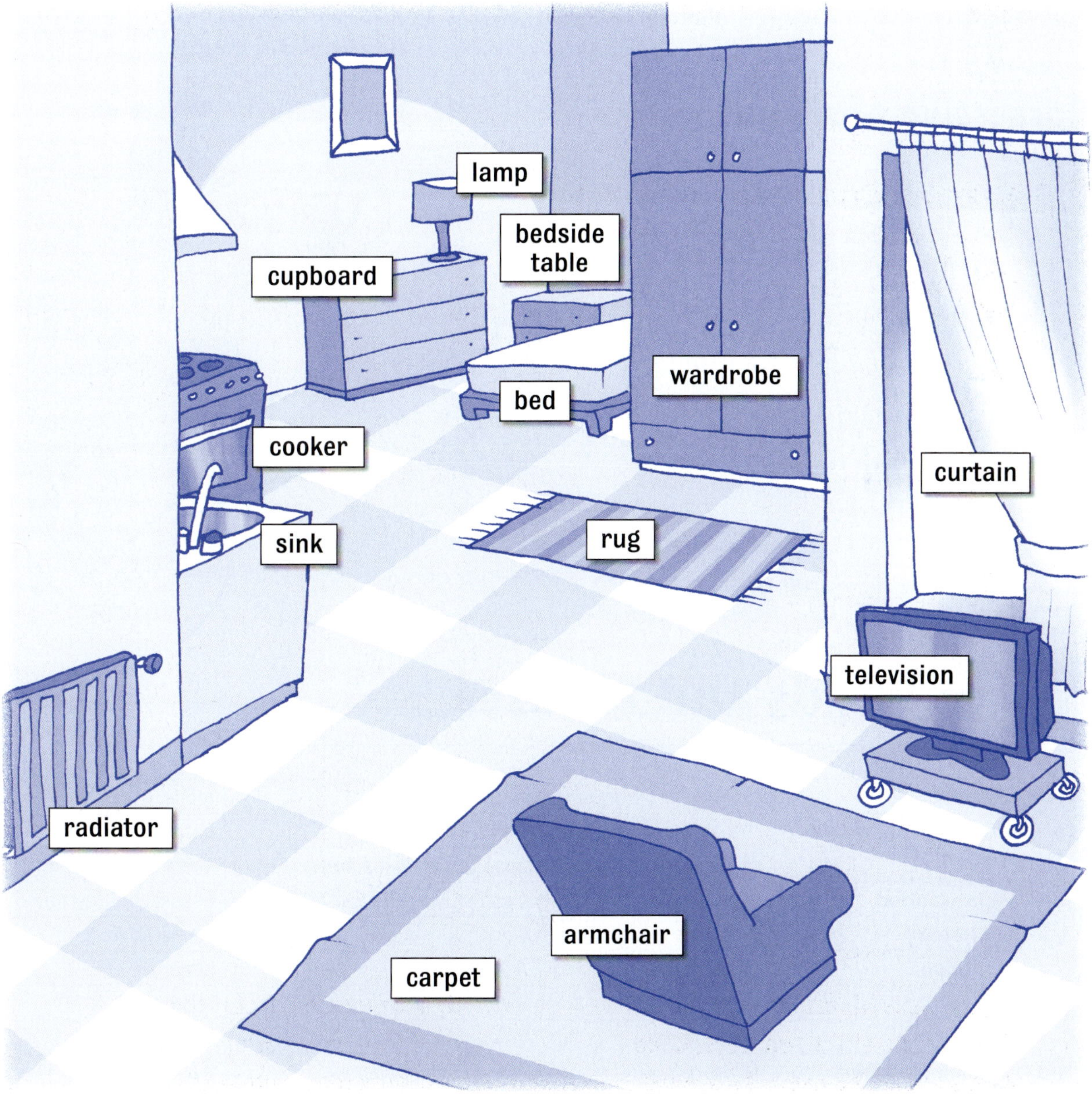

SB p. 104

Different homes

Possessive pronouns

MORE Words and Phrases

1	**cheap**	*I bought some cheap shoes in town yesterday.*	billig
	tired of	*I'm tired of playing football. Let's go home.*	müde, überdrüssig
	underneath	*The cat is underneath the table.*	unter(halb)
3	fridge	*I have to go shopping because our fridge is empty.*	Kühlschrank
7	**conversation**	*I had an interesting conversation with Joe last night.*	Gespräch, Unterhaltung
8	**dictionary**	*This word is not in my dictionary.*	Wörterbuch
	next door	*The people next door are friendly.*	nebenan
	share	*I want to share my lunch with you.*	teilen
	whose	*Whose computer is this? It's not mine!*	wessen
11	**washing machine**	*All my dirty clothes are in the washing machine.*	Waschmaschine

UNIT 15 Feeling better

Essential Vocabulary

1 **Match the words with the picture. Draw lines.**

headache | throat | illness | ankle | stomach ache | oxygen | toe

More Vocabulary

2 **Do the crossword.**

DOWN:

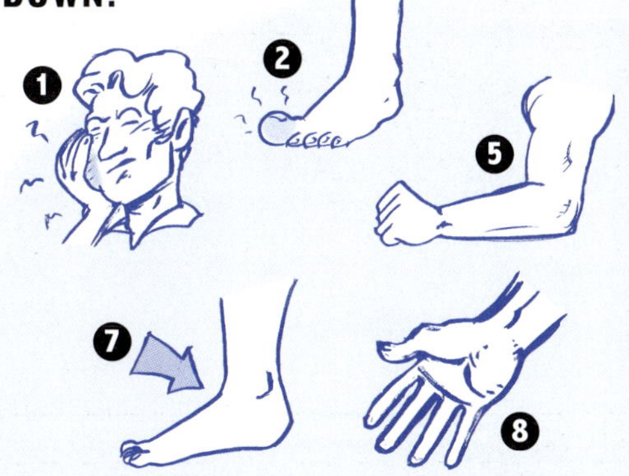

ACROSS:

SB p. 107

Reading and Writing

3 Here are some more "doctor, doctor" jokes. Match them with the endings.

1	**Patient**	Doctor, doctor. I think I'm a bell.	☐	**Doctor**	Sit!
2	**Patient**	Doctor, doctor. I think I'm invisible*.	☐	**Doctor**	Take the legs off your bed!
3	**Patient**	Doctor, doctor. I dream there are monsters under my bed. What can I do?	☐	**Doctor**	Take these and if it doesn't help give me a ring!
4	**Patient**	Doctor, doctor. I feel like a dog!	☐	**Doctor**	Next!

VOCABULARY: *invisible – unsichtbar

4 Write the words in the correct order to complete the doctor's conversations.

1 **Doctor** you / How / today / are / ?
How are you today? ....

Amanda ankle / My / bit. / hurts / a
....

2 **Doctor** your / Does / hurt / leg / ?
....

Bartholomew knee. / it's / No, / my / just
....

3 **Doctor** matter / What's / the / ?
....

Sebastian a / back. / my / I've / got / in / pain
....

4 **Doctor** you / better / today / Do / feel / ?
....

Fatima headache. / No, / a / got / still / I've
....

5 Read the notes and write the names next to the pictures.

Dear Ms Jones,
I'm sorry but Jimmy can't come to school today because he can't find his pet snake. Now he has to look for it.

Dear Mr Cartwright,
Michael can't come to school – he has a very bad stomach ache. The doctor says he must stay at home.

Dear Ms Hamilton,
Please excuse my son Gordon from school for the next few days. He is on his way to Hollywood because he wants to be a film star.

....

....

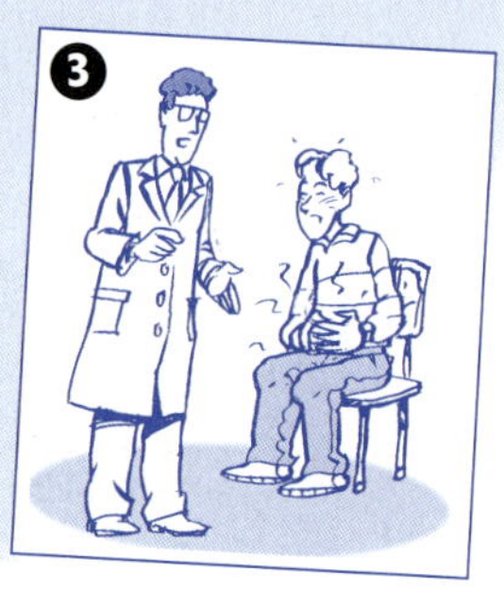

....

SB p. 106, 107

6 Imagine you are a parent. Write two notes for children who cannot go to school.

Dear .... ,	....
Please excuse my	....
....	....
He/She	....
....	....

7 CHOICES

A Put the numbers in the correct places. Then check in the Student's Book on page 109. There are two numbers you don't need.

10,000,000 500 20 2,000 20,000 25 200,000

1 The Amazon Rainforest produces ....% of the world's oxygen.
2 Over .... plants in the rainforest can help against cancer.
3 These days there are only about .... Indians in the Amazon.
4 There were about .... Indians in the Amazon Rainforest – but that was .... years ago.

B Complete the text. Use the pictures to help you.

The Amazon [1]...................................... in South America is in the middle of a rainforest. There is a big problem in the rainforest – people cut down the [2]...................................... because they want to make a lot of [3]...................................... very quickly. They also cut down the trees so that they have more land for their [4]...................................... . The Amazon is a very important place for three reasons. First, it is the home to lots of animals, birds, reptiles and insects. Second, it is the place where a lot of the world's oxygen comes from. Third, there are thousands of [5]...................................... that are important for making [6]...................................... that can help against illnesses like cancer. Indian medicine men know how to use the plants to make the medicines. But now there are not very many medicine men, and they are very old. It is important for the [7]...................................... that we learn what they know!

SB p. 109

Essential Grammar Present perfect / Past participles

8 Match the sentences and pictures.

- ☐ He has fallen off his bike.
- ☐ She has walked into a lamp post.
- ☐ I've cut my leg.
- ☐ I've eaten too much!
- ☐ She has hurt her back.
- ☐ He has hurt his toe.
- ☐ I think I've broken my ankle.

9 Complete the table.

verb	past simple	past participle
go	went	gone
eat		
have		
do		
want		
play		
see		
think		
ask		
watch		
sit		
drink		

SB p. 108

More Grammar Present perfect / Past participles

10 Find nine more past participles. (← → ↑ ↓ ↘)

T	O	P	B	R	O	K	E	N
H	H	A	F	T	E	N	A	R
E	S	O	O	T	N	O	P	O
R	T	R	U	H	N	W	N	C
E	R	O	N	G	O	N	E	Y
T	A	H	D	U	H	G	L	P
H	Y	T	L	O	S	T	L	E
A	E	F	E	B	E	E	A	L
B	R	O	K	N	E	F	F	S

broken

....

....

....

....

....

....

....

....

....

11 Complete the sentences with the present perfect form of the verb.

1 I think I .... my leg. (break)
2 We .... our cat. (lose)
3 Dad .... his car. (crash)
4 You .... your money. (drop)
5 I .... my homework. (finish)
6 Mrs Green .... an accident. (have)
7 They .... house again. (move)
8 He .... a prize. (win)

12 Read Rachel's email and complete with the verbs in the box.

passed
broken
bought
gone
fallen
met

From: rachel123@homenet.co.uk
Subject: news about my family

REPLY

Hi Arnold,

How are things? I hope you're well. I'm writing with all the news about our family. Do you remember my brother Joshua? He has [1].......... a guitar and now he plays music really loudly all the time. He wants to start a rock band! My dad has [2].......... his arm. He went to sleep on the sofa and fell off! He can't go to work so he's very sad. My aunt and uncle have [3].......... on holiday – to Iceland! My sister Patricia has [4].......... her driving test. Now she drives round and round the town – she never stops! My other brother, Hamilton, has [5].......... a girl from Japan and has [6].......... in love with her. Now he's learning the language – he wants to go and live in Tokyo!

And me? Well, I'm going to leave home. My family are completely mad!

Lots of love,
Rachel

SB p. 110, 111

13 Read Rachel's email in 12 again and write the names of the people under the pictures.

1 ....

2 ....

3 ....

4 ....

5 ....

14 Complete with the correct form of one of the verbs in the box.

break
eat
pass
want
go
fall

1 There's nothing left. The dog .... it all.

2 I .... my tests!

3 Sorry, Jane isn't here. She .... into town.

4 I think I .... my toe.

5 Dad! Quickly! Jimmy .... out of the tree!

6 Oh, thanks, Grandma. I .... always .... one of these.

15 Match the sentence halves.

1 I've fixed
2 I've read
3 I've done
4 I've broken

☐ two books.
☐ my bike.
☐ my arm.
☐ all my homework.

5 I've bought
6 I've been
7 I've met
8 I've fallen

☐ out of a tree.
☐ an interesting boy.
☐ a new dress.
☐ to a party.

16 What about you? Write down eight things you've done this week.

SB p. 111

WORD FILE

Aches and pains

MORE Words and Phrases

1	chart	*On the chart you can see all the names and numbers.*	Tabelle
	medicine	*John wants to study medicine at university.*	Medizin
	memory	*Her memory is very good. She can remember lots of important facts.*	Gedächtnis
	vote	*Don't forget to vote for your favourite star!*	wählen
6	**drop**	*Don't drop that apple!*	fallen lassen
	That's a shame.		Wie schade!
10	clear away	*Big machines clear away the trees.*	wegräumen
	company	*Alan works for a big company in America.*	Gesellschaft; Firma
	Indian	*The Indians in the rainforest know a lot about plants.*	Indio (Ureinwohner Südamerikas)
	less (than)	*It takes less than ten minutes to get there.*	weniger (als)
	produce	*We produce mobile phones here.*	erzeugen
	rainforest	*The rainforest is a wonderful place.*	Regenwald
	sick	*I was sick yesterday.*	krank
	type	*What type of holiday do you like?*	Art; Typ; Sorte
	valuable	*Plants in the rainforest are very valuable for science.*	wertvoll
	wildlife	*The rainforest is home to a lot of wildlife.*	Tierwelt; in freier Natur lebende Tiere
11	consequence	*The consequences of the war were very bad for everyone.*	Folge
14	**injure**	*He injured his legs in the accident.*	verletzen
	writer	*Who wrote the message? Who is the writer?*	Verfasser/in
G	**lose**	*I've lost my cat.*	verlieren
	pass (a test)	*I want to pass this test!*	(eine Prüfung) bestehen
DVD	Let's see ...		Mal schauen ...
	Who cares?		Wen interessiert's?, Na und?
	I have no clue.		Ich habe keine Ahnung.

UNIT 16 Light rain in the north

Essential Vocabulary

1 Complete the words.

y ~~ny~~ y dy iny gy ld ot storm

1 sun ny ....
2 thunder..........
3 snow..........
4 wind..........
5 clou..........
6 ra..........
7 h..........
8 fog..........
9 co..........

2 Write the words from 1 under the pictures.

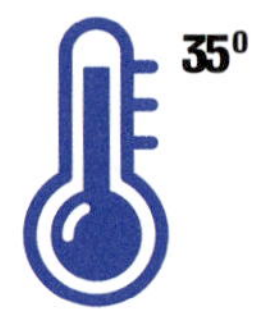

1 .... 2 .... 3 .... 4 .... 5 ....

6 .... 7 .... 8 .... 9 ....

More Vocabulary

3 Find the nine weather words in the wordsearch. (← → ↑ ↓)

F	E	O	Q	S	C	O	L	D	R	S	R
E	O	I	U	L	A	E	A	T	U	E	A
Y	G	G	O	F	F	H	O	T	I	G	I
B	A	H	S	E	I	E	X	Q	Y	T	R
O	S	K	C	P	F	G	C	N	O	S	Y
K	D	O	L	D	U	H	N	S	K	A	D
L	Y	O	O	Y	K	U	O	N	L	Z	N
O	N	W	U	N	S	O	P	O	I	C	I
O	I	W	D	N	O	I	I	W	I	D	W
R	A	A	Y	U	O	L	O	Y	H	S	J
M	R	O	T	S	R	E	D	N	U	H	T

SB p. 114

4 Match the words with their definitions.

1	weather report	☐	how hot or cold something is
2	weatherman / weatherwoman	☐	information (e.g. on TV) about what the weather will be like
3	temperature	☐	a short rainfall
4	the weather clears up	☐	without clouds
5	clear (adjective)	☐	not hot, not cold
6	shower	☐	someone who presents tomorrow's weather (on TV)
7	wet	☐	the weather becomes better
8	mild	☐	full of water (opposite of dry)

Reading and Writing

5 Look at the map and write the weather forecast.

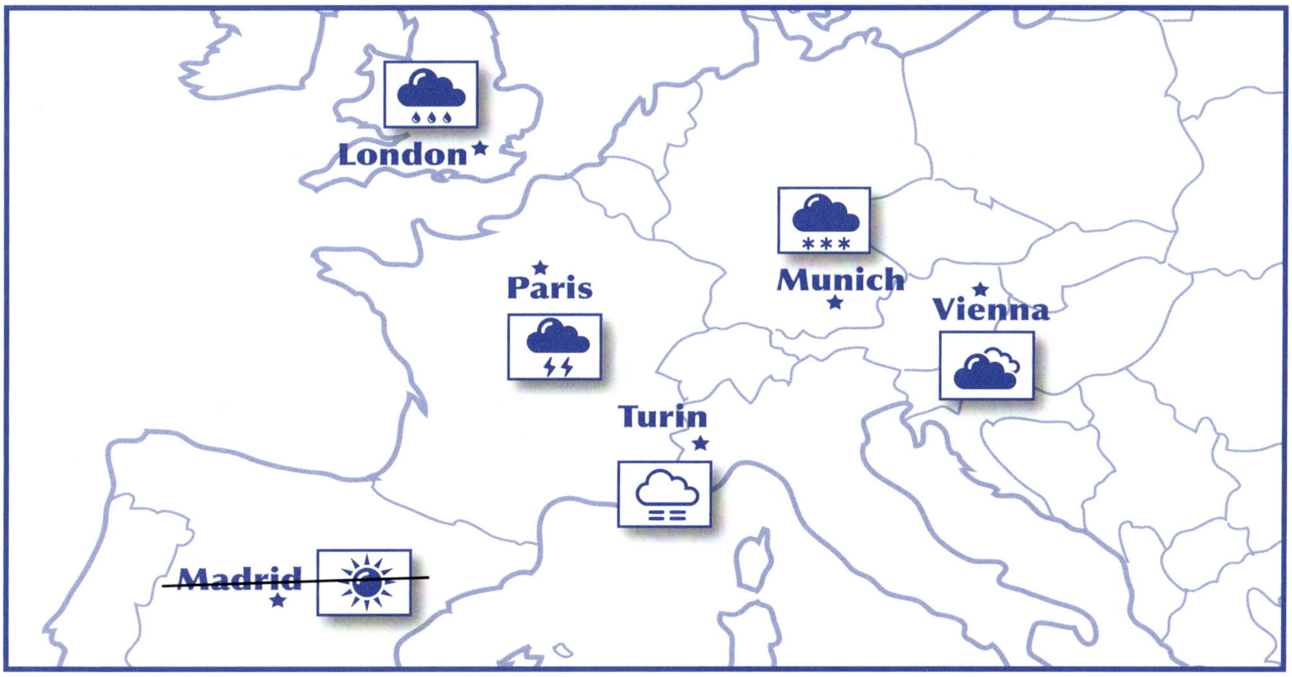

1 It will be sunny in Madrid. ....
2 ....
3 ....
4 ....
5 ....
6 ....

6 Remember the formula. Tick T (*True*) or F (*False*) for the sentences.

To convert Fahrenheit temperatures into Centigrade:

$$(°F - 32) \times \frac{5}{9} = °C$$

- Begin by subtracting* 32 from the Fahrenheit number.
- Divide* the answer by 9.
- Then multiply* that answer by 5.

VOCABULARY
***subtract** – subtrahieren;
divide – dividieren;
multiply – multiplizieren

1	100°C is hotter than 200°F.	T ☐	F ☐
2	86°F is colder than 25°C.	T ☐	F ☐
3	122°F is the same as 60°C.	T ☐	F ☐
4	30°C is not as hot as 94°F.	T ☐	F ☐
5	40°F is not as cold as 10°C.	T ☐	F ☐
6	0°C is as cold as 32°F.	T ☐	F ☐

SB p. 114, 115, 116

A Read the story and choose the best title for it. Then tick T (*True*) or F (*False*).

A hot day   Friends in the park   Rain and sun

....

When I was six years old, I was in the back garden of our house with my friends. We were playing football. It was sunny. Then I saw some black clouds in the sky. I went around the house. There was the washing on the line*. I said to my mum, "It'll be rainy soon." At that moment it started to rain. I quickly helped my mum take the washing off the line. Then I went back to my friends in the back garden. It was sunny. I went back to the front garden – rain! Strange! When I looked one way, it was sun. When I looked the other way, it was rain! (Jamie, 13)

VOCABULARY: ***line** – Wäscheleine

1 The story is about a time when Jamie was 13 years old. T ☐ F ☐
2 Jamie was playing football in the back garden. T ☐ F ☐
3 There was the washing on the line on the other side of the house. T ☐ F ☐
4 Jamie's friends helped his mother. T ☐ F ☐
5 It was raining on both sides of the house. T ☐ F ☐

B Read the story and choose the best title for it. Then answer the questions.

The water went away   Buying sandbags   When I was twelve

....

I was about 12. There was a river at the end of our garden. On a Thursday in October, it started to rain and rain. On Saturday morning, I went into the garden and I saw that the river was higher than usual. The water started to come into our garden and I shouted to my mum and dad. They ran out, and my dad went to get some sandbags*. But at that moment the rain stopped and the water began to go back again. My dad came back and we watched the water go away. We were so happy, and the three of us laughed and danced around. (Simon, 14)

VOCABULARY: ***sandbag** – Sandsack

1 Why did Simon shout to his parents?

....

2 What did Simon's dad do when he saw what the problem was?

....

3 What happened in the end?

....

SB p. 117, 118

Essential Grammar *will*-future

8 Complete the sentences with the missing verbs.

rain
do
drive
meet
finish
help
go
tell

1 Here. I'll .... you with your homework.
2 The weather's not good. I think it'll .... later.
3 One day, I'll .... around in a Ferrari. One day!
4 I'll .... you outside the cinema at 8 p.m., OK?
5 I'm feeling tired. I think I'll .... to bed.
6 I'm bored. I won't .... any more work tonight.
7 It's a secret. Promise you won't .... anybody.
8 It's a long job. We won't .... before midnight.

9 Write the sentences in the correct speech bubbles.

I'll give you some.
Oh! It really hurts.
I'm really scared of dogs.
I've got lots of homework tonight.
I haven't got enough money.
I'll bring it tomorrow. I promise.
OK, leave it. I'll do it later.
I'll carry it for you.
~~Where's your homework?~~
I'll take you to hospital.
I'm not. I'll get it.
This suitcase* is heavy.

VOCABULARY: *suitcase – Koffer

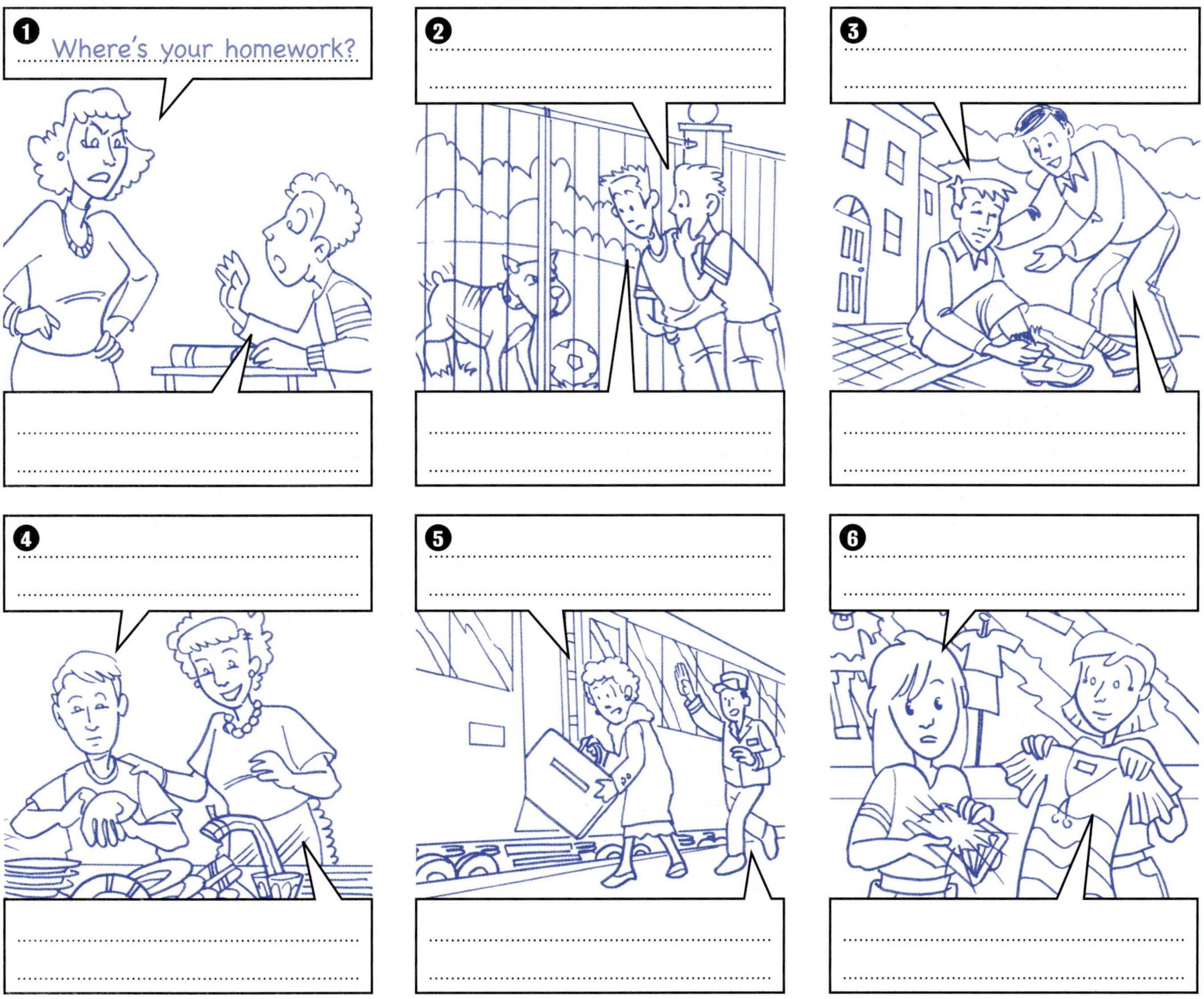

SB p. 116, 119

Essential Grammar *will*

10 **Look at the pictures. Then put the words in the correct order to make sentences.**

1 anyone / I / it. / buy / don't / will / think

....

2 today. / think / coat / need / my / I / I'll

....

3 you'll / test / is / The / and / easy / pass. / very

....

4 on / sleep / You'll / well / bed. / very / this

....

5 berries / make / Those / sick / you / will.

....

6 gold / so / It's / expensive / will / it / be.

....

More Grammar *will / won't / might*

11 **Match the pictures and the sentences.**

- ☐ It won't hurt.
- ☐ It won't bite you.
- ☐ I won't be home for dinner.
- ☐ I won't pass.
- ☐ She won't phone me.
- ☐ You won't wear it.

1

2

3

4

5

6

SB p. 119

12 Match the sentences.

1	It's my birthday tomorrow.	☐	I'll close the window.
2	The film starts at six. Don't forget!	☐	I won't tell anybody.
3	How am I going to get home?	☐	OK. I'll record it for you.
4	The car's really dirty.	☐	Thanks. I'll give it back to you tomorrow.
5	Here's £3.	☐	I'll answer it.
6	I'm going to miss the game on TV.	1	I'll make a cake.
7	I'm really hungry.	☐	Don't worry – I'll be there.
8	It's cold in here.	☐	I'll clean it for you.
9	The phone's ringing.	☐	I'll make you a sandwich.
10	It's a secret.	☐	My dad will take you in our car.

13 Look at the pictures and write the people's dreams.

1 *I'll be rich one day.* ....

2 ....

3 ....

4 ....

5 ....

6 ....

14 Complete with your own ideas.

1 **A** The party starts at eight, Dave.
B I know but I'll be a bit late because …

2 **A** Lunch will be ready in an hour.
B OK, so I won't …

3 **A** What's Mike going to do when he finishes school?
B He's not sure yet, but I think he'll …

4 **A** What chance have Manchester United got in the cup final?
B They won't win because …

5 **A** Where are you going on holiday this year?
B I'm not sure but it won't …

6 **A** I only slept two hours last night.
B Well, you will …

SB p. 119

15 **Write sentences about your future. Use *might*, *might not*, *'ll* or *won't* and the ideas in the box.**

buy a laptop
go to the moon
travel to the Amazon
learn to drive
be a famous scientist
write a book

....
....
....
....
....
....

WORD FILE

Weather forecast

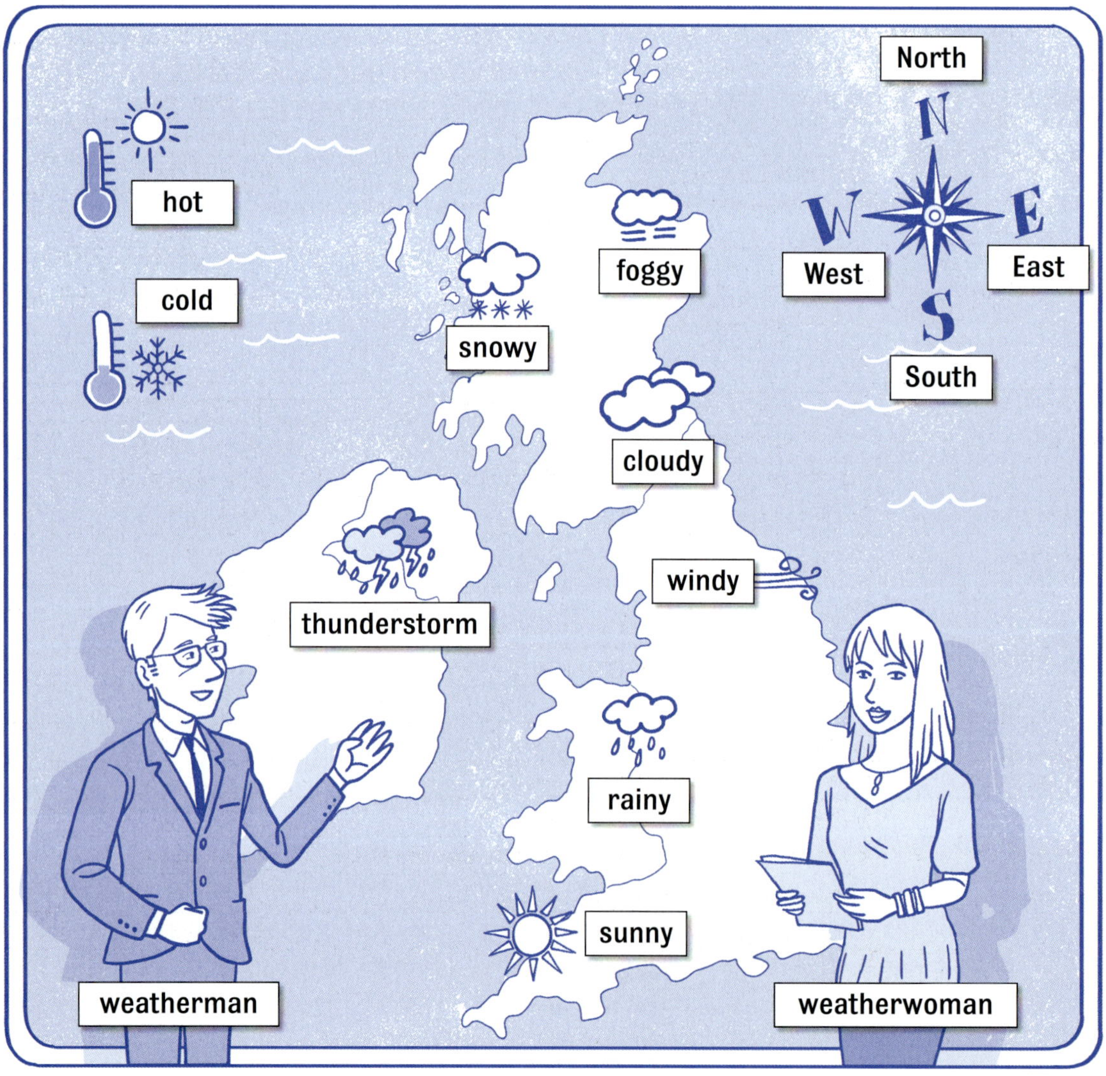

SB p. 119

MORE Words and Phrases

1	**coast**	*It lives off the coast of Australia.*	Küste
	continue	*The rain will continue until tomorrow.*	andauern; weitergehen
	cool	*It's warm during the day, but quite cool at night.*	kühl
	dry	*We had very dry weather for our holidays last year.*	trocken
	formula	*The formula is C = (F-32):1.8.*	Formel
	give way	*Rain in the morning will give way to sun later on.*	ausweichen, Platz machen
	scale	*On a scale from 1 to 10: How good was your day?*	Skala, Maßstab
	temperature	*The temperature fell to below zero last night.*	Temperatur
3	**clear up**	*The bad weather will clear up by this evening.*	aufklaren
	forecast	*The forecast is very good for tomorrow.*	Vorhersage
	outlook	*The outlook for the weekend is warm and sunny.*	Aussicht, Ausblick
	thick	*Watch out! There's thick fog here.*	dick, dicht
4	all day	*It will be sunny all day in England.*	den ganzen Tag
	fog	*Heavy fog in the Stoke area will clear up later.*	Nebel
	Have a nice day!		Einen schönen Tag noch!
	make sure	*Make sure you take your umbrella!*	sich versichern, darauf achten
	rise	*The temperatures will rise to 20°C.*	steigen
	weather report	*The weather report will be on TV at 8 o'clock.*	Wetterbericht
5	**hiking**	*We went hiking in the mountains.*	wandern
	lovely	*What a lovely surprise! Thank you!*	schön
	pretty	*I was pretty surprised to hear the news.*	ziemlich
	promise	*I promise to come and help you tomorrow.*	versprechen
7	**apologise**	*I apologise – I was wrong.*	sich entschuldigen
	bathing suit	*Bring your bathing suit with you.*	Badeanzug
	pack	*Pack your bags! We're going on holiday!*	packen
	raincoat	*It's raining. Take your raincoat.*	Regenmantel
	shower	*There will be showers – bring an umbrella!*	Regenschauer
	situation	*The situation is difficult.*	Situation, Lage
	swimming trunks	*Have you packed your swimming trunks?*	Badehose
	turn off/on	*Jamie, turn off the TV.*	etwas aus-/einschalten
	turn up/down	*Turn up the volume – I can't hear the music.*	aufdrehen / leiser drehen
	unpack	*Unpack your bathing suit and pack your raincoat!*	auspacken
	volume	*Please don't turn up the volume.*	Lautstärke
	wherever	*There will be sunshine wherever we look.*	wo auch immer
10	**average**	*The average temperature this week will be around 15°C.*	durchschnittlich
	below	*The temperature will be below 0°C tomorrow.*	unten; unterhalb
	convert	*Try to convert Fahrenheit to Celsius.*	umrechnen
	generally	*It's generally hot and sunny in Italy in the summer.*	allgemein
	inch (pl inches)	*An inch is about two and a half centimetres.*	Zoll (2,54 cm)
	mile	*I live ten miles from here.*	Meile
	mild	*The forecast is for a really mild day tomorrow.*	mild
	rainfall	*The rainfall in the Amazon Rainforest can be very heavy.*	Niederschlag
	record	*He recorded a time of 15 minutes for his last race.*	aufzeichnen
	sea level	*Death Valley is 282 feet below sea level.*	Meeresspiegel
	starting point	*Sally's house was the starting point for our trip.*	Ausgangspunkt
	throughout the year	*In the Lake District it can be rainy throughout the year.*	im ganzen Jahr
	wet	*All my clothes are wet because of the rain.*	nass
11	tan	*You have a great tan.*	(Sonnen-)Bräune

UNIT 17 Get active!

Essential Vocabulary

1 Number the words.

- ☐ ice skating
- ☐ yachtswoman
- ☐ bike
- ☐ windsurfing
- ☐ roller-skating
- 1 climbing
- ☐ trainer
- ☐ sportsman
- ☐ score
- ☐ goalie
- ☐ yacht
- ☐ cycling
- ☐ race
- ☐ sailing
- ☐ climber
- ☐ kick
- ☐ sportswoman

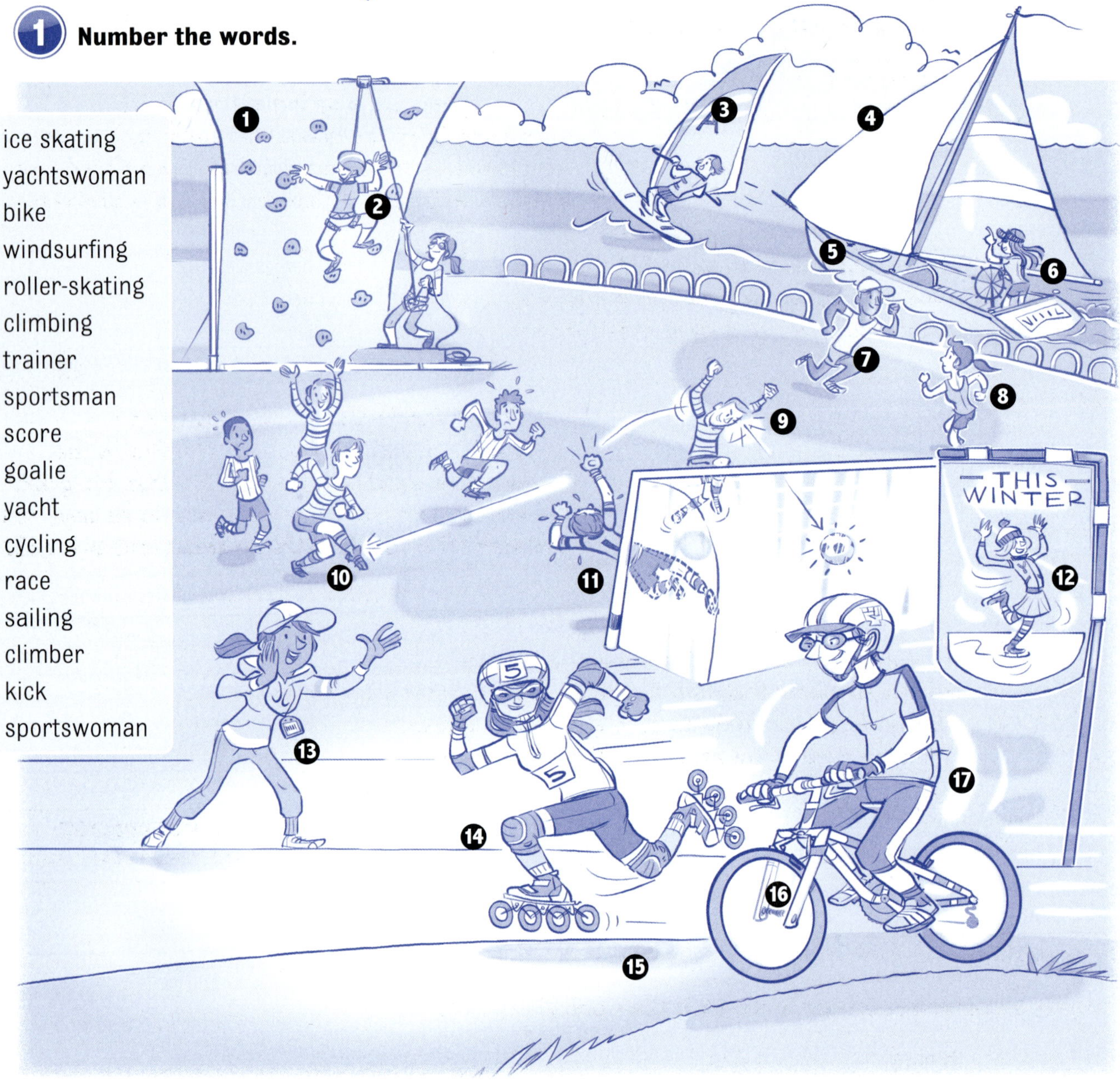

More Vocabulary

2 Find the odd one out.

1 football tennis basketball volleyball

2 surfing swimming running windsurfing

3 sailing cycling swimming snowboarding

4 skiing football mountain climbing snowboarding

5 skateboarding snowboarding surfing ice skating

SB p. 120

3 Which sport(s) are they talking about?

1 I usually play in the summer – it's too cold in the winter. It's good because you only need two people. But sometimes you can play with four people, of course.

....

2 I love this sport! You can play indoors but I like playing it on the beach. All you need is a net and a ball – but even on the beach you need four people to play. But that isn't usually a problem.

....

3 This is the best sport in the world because all you need is a pair of good trainers and off you go! No special equipment* and you don't even need other people!

....

4 The first time I did this sport I hated it because I got so cold! But in the summer the weather is warmer and then it's great to be in the warm water! I go with my friends now, at the weekends. The board's a bit expensive, but that's all.

....

5 My favourite sport is a problem for me because there aren't any mountains where I live. So I have to go to another country. And I can only do it in winter! It's difficult and the boards are expensive, but I still love it!

....

VOCABULARY
***equipment** – Ausrüstung

Reading and Writing

4 Complete the dialogue with the words in the box.

tennis
twice
favourite
game
often
sports

Nicole	What's your 1.................................. sport, Matthew?
Matthew	Hmm, probably basketball. But I like 2.................................. too.
Nicole	Are you a good player?
Matthew	I'm not bad.
Nicole	How 3.................................. do you play?
Matthew	Well, I play tennis 4.................................. a week and basketball four times a week. I'm in the school team.
Nicole	Oh really? You do a lot of sport!
Matthew	True. What about you? Do you like any 5.................................. ?
Nicole	Well, I like watching basketball on TV.
Matthew	So, would you like to watch tomorrow's 6.................................. with me?
Nicole	Sure. Why not?

SB p. 120, 121

5 CHOICES

A **Read the story and put the sentences in the correct order.**

Coach* Carter

Last week, I saw a film called *Coach Carter*. It's about a basketball team at Richmond High School* in the USA, who lose most of their games. And then they get a new coach – a man called Mr Carter. He makes them work very hard, they have to practise every day. And then they win some games, so they're very happy! And everything seems OK, but there's a problem: the players are also at school and they aren't working very much so they don't get good grades*. And Mr Carter locks the school gym*! Now the players can't practise. The headmaster* of the school thinks Carter is wrong and he opens the gym again. The boys can play and practise again, and the team gets to the big final – but they lose to St Francis School: 70–68 in a very exciting game. The players are very unhappy, but Coach Carter thinks they have done very well and he congratulates them. It's not a bad story.

VOCABULARY
***coach** – Trainer/in;
high school – Oberstufengymnasium;
grade – Note;
gym – Turnhalle;
headmaster – Schulleiter

- [ ] But then their grades were not good any more.
- [1] The basketball team of Richmond High wasn't very good.
- [ ] The team lost the big final, but their coach was happy.
- [ ] Then they got a new coach.
- [ ] So their coach locked the gym.
- [ ] The students practised every day.
- [ ] But the headmaster opened it again.

B **Put the text about Emma Sanderson in the correct order.**

- [ ] she was five, her family bought a house in Helensborough,
- [ ] was eleven she already started winning competitions. She
- [1] Emma Sanderson, from England, is a yachtswoman. When
- [ ] later sailed a yacht, in team races or alone. She won the
- [ ] her sailing. Emma is married and has a daughter.
- [ ] complete the 29,000 mile solo race, and she was alone at
- [ ] 25, but she is most famous for winning the Around Alone
- [ ] Scotland. That was an ideal place for sailing. When she
- [ ] Race in 2002/03. She was the youngest woman to
- [ ] Round Britain and Ireland Race in 2000, when she was
- [ ] sea for 132 days. Now Emma enjoys telling children about

SB p. 123

6 Read the text about Tommy Caldwell again on page 124 of your Student's Book and complete the notes.

Name: 1 ....

Nationality: 2 ....

Profession: 3 ....

What he has already achieved:

4 ....

....

Why he loves his job:

5 ....

....

Dangers of his job:

6 ....

....

Ambitions:

7 ....

....

Essential Grammar Present perfect with *already* and *yet*

7 Match the pictures with the sentences.

1 She has already got the trophy*.
2 They haven't phoned her yet.
3 She hasn't found the answer yet.
4 She has already phoned for help.
5 The mechanic* hasn't fixed* her car yet.
6 She hasn't got the trophy yet.

VOCABULARY
***trophy** – Pokal; **mechanic** – Mechaniker/in; **fix** – reparieren

SB p. 124

Essential Grammar Present perfect with *ever* and *never*

8 **Match the questions and answers.**

1 Have you ever met anybody famous?
2 Have you ever been on television?
3 Have you ever been to the sea?
4 Have you ever written a poem?
5 Have you ever won a competition?
6 Have you ever gone snowboarding?
7 Have you ever fallen asleep in a lesson?
8 Have you ever seen a ghost?

☐ No, I never have – and I'm never going to! I hate mountains and snow!
☐ Well, I met a footballer in a shop once, but I can't say he was really famous.
☐ Once. But the teacher didn't see me so it was OK.
☐ No, I haven't. But my mum has. She was really scared.
☐ Yes, I have. Two years ago I won the tennis competition at school!
☐ Yes, I have. And I love reading them, too.
☐ Yes, I have. We went swimming every day.
☐ No, but my sister has. She was on a quiz programme once. She lost!

More Grammar Present perfect with *already* and *yet*

9 **Write the questions using *already* or *yet*. Then match the questions and answers.**

1 he / do his homework
Has he done his homework yet? [g] No he hasn't. He's still working it out.
2 you / see the new Indiana Jones film
.... ☐ ....
3 we / arrive
.... ☐ ....
4 you / lose your coat
.... ☐ ....
5 Harriet's dog / have puppies*
.... ☐ ....
6 she / get a new boyfriend
.... ☐ ....
7 they / eat all of their vegetables
.... ☐ ....
8 Dad / finish cooking dinner
.... ☐ ....

a) No, they haven't, so don't give them any ice cream.
b) No, I haven't. Is it on already?
c) Yes, he has. We can eat in 10 minutes.
d) Yes, I have. I'm wearing my sister's.
e) Another 10 minutes, then we're there.
f) Yes, she has. His name's Bernie.
g) No he hasn't. He's still working it out.
h) Yes, she has. Do you want one?

VOCABULARY: ***puppy** – Welpe

SB p. 121, 122, 125

More Grammar Present perfect with *ever* and *never*

10 Write the words in the correct order to make sentences or questions.

1 you / have / handball / ever / played / ?
Have you ever played handball?

2 Japanese* / eaten / you / have / food / ever / ?

3 never / I've / Olympic Games / to / been / the / .

4 ever / you / broken / arm / have / your / ?

5 competition / never / I've / a / won / .

6 brother / my / a / poem / never / has / written / .

7 parents / never / my / have / France / to / been / .

8 dinner / family / you / ever / have / for / your / cooked / ?

VOCABULARY: *Japanese – japanisch

Developing speaking competencies

11 Match the requests and offers with the replies.

1 Can you phone James?
2 Could you make me a sandwich?
3 I'll take the dog for a walk.
4 Why don't I talk to Jane?

☐ Sure, no problem. Cheese or ham?
☐ Fantastic. He really needs one.
☐ Of course. I'll call him in the morning.
☐ That's a great idea! She always listens to you.

12 Write offers or requests to complete the dialogues.

1 **Viv** ……
Ian Sure, no problem. I can buy some on my way home from school.

2 **Rob** ……
Liz Fantastic. I'm finding it really difficult.

3 **Tim** ……
Deb Of course. It's getting quite cold in here.

4 **Jim** ……
Baz That's great. They're really heavy.

SB p. 125, 126

WORD FILE

Sports

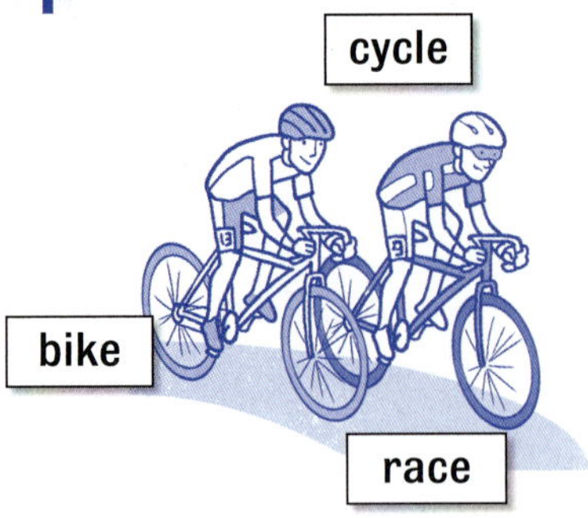

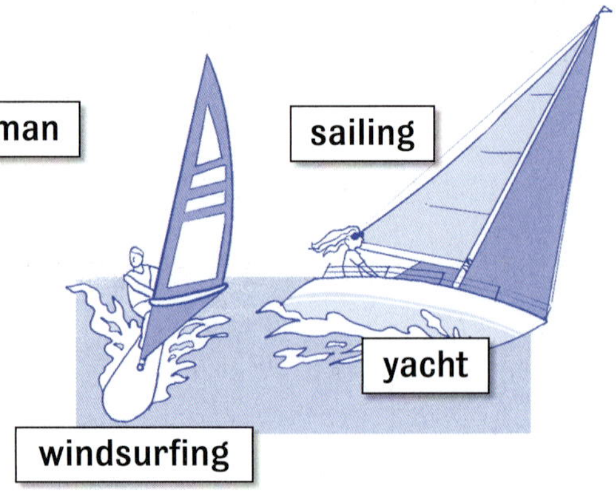

MORE Words and Phrases

4	**grow up**	*When I grow up I want to be an Olympic skier.*	erwachsen werden; aufwachsen
	profile	*Her profile describes her as a surfer in California.*	Profil, Porträt
5	**competition**	*I love taking part in competitions!*	Wettbewerb
	ever	*Have you ever played volleyball?*	je(mals)
	get lost	*They went into the forest and got lost.*	sich verirren
7	**appear**	*Suddenly a ghost appeared.*	erscheinen
	fall asleep	*My dad always falls asleep in front of the TV.*	einschlafen
8	nil	*In the end the score was two – nil.*	null
	rest	*I needed some rest.*	Ruhe; Pause
	tackle	*Helen tackled Eddie.*	attackieren, niederrennen (im Sport)
	waste of time	*I've had enough. It's a waste of time.*	Zeitverschwendung
10	challenge	*A race around the world is a big challenge.*	Herausforderung
	cliff	*He climbed up the cliff from the beach.*	Klippe, Felsen
	education	*You get your education at school … and at home!*	Bildung; Erziehung
	extreme	*The weather at sea can be extreme sometimes.*	extrem
	face something	*Emma had to face many dangers on her trip.*	sich etwas aussetzen
	former	*She went to visit one of her former teachers last week.*	ehemalig
	full	*His biggest wish is to live a full and happy life.*	erfüllend; ausgefüllt
	hurricane	*The hurricane hit Florida and destroyed many houses.*	Orkan; Hurrikan
	obsessed	*He was obsessed by his wish to climb mountains.*	besessen
	ocean	*The oceans cover $^2/_3$ of the Earth.*	Meer, Ozean
	sail	*She wants to sail around the world again.*	segeln
	thrill	*Climbing is a big thrill for Tommy.*	Nervenkitzel
	top	*He climbed to the top of the mountain.*	Gipfel; Spitze
	yachtswoman	*She is a yachtswoman and sailed around the world.*	Seglerin
11	**make friends**	*Volleyball is a good way to make friends.*	Freundschaft schließen
	professional	*I want to play professional basketball.*	professionell; hauptberuflich

SWYK Units 13–17

UNIT 18 Caring for animals

Essential Vocabulary

1 Match the pictures and the phrases. Write numbers.

- ☐ take your pet to the vet
- ☐ feed your pet
- ☐ stroke your pet
- ☐ brush your pet
- ☐ give your pet a bath
- ☐ clean out the litter tray
- ☐ dry your pet
- ☐ clean out your pet's cage
- ☐ play with your pet
- ☐ walk your pet

More Vocabulary

2 Complete the sentences.

1 Susie is ....stroking.......... her pet.

2 Susie is .... her pet.

3 Susie is .... her pet's cage.

4 Susie is .... her pet.

5 Susie is .... her pet.

SB p. 128

Reading and Writing

3 Complete the dialogue with the sentences from the box.

Yes, their names are Clever and Smart.
No, they sleep in a box in my room.
Yes, that's right.
Yes, two rats.
Yes, I do. When I come home from school we play for half an hour.
Yes, they do. Sometimes they come to sleep in my bed.

Interviewer Have you got a pet, Ruby?
Ruby 1 ....
Interviewer Rats?
Ruby 2 ....
Interviewer So your rats are very intelligent.
Ruby 3 ....
Interviewer Do the rats sleep in a cage?
Ruby 4 ....
Interviewer Don't they run around at night?
Ruby 5 ....
Interviewer Do you spend a lot of time with them?
Ruby 6 ....

4 Read the interview and write the questions.

How often do you feed it?
What does it eat?
And where does it live?
Where does it come from?
And what colour is it?
Is it a difficult pet to keep?

My pet

Interviewer Daniel, you've got an unusual pet. Tell us more about it.

Daniel It's a chameleon.

Interviewer Wow, a chameleon. 1 ....

Daniel Chameleons live in many different countries but mine comes from Madagascar.

Interviewer 2 ....

Daniel It's usually green but when it gets angry it changes colour to red. It can change colour to orange and yellow, too. But I don't know why.

Interviewer 3 ....

Daniel No. It's quite easy really. I mean you don't have to give it a bath or anything like that. You just have to give it food and clean its glass tank once a week.

Interviewer 4 ....

Daniel Just once a day.

Interviewer 5 ....

Daniel Insects and things like that.

Interviewer 6 ....

Daniel In a big glass tank. It's about two metres high and one metre wide. It has got a tree in it.

SB p. 129

5 **Read the interview again and tick T (*True*) or F (*False*).**

1 You can only find chameleons in Madagascar. T ☐ F ☐
2 Daniel's chameleon changes to red when it's angry. T ☐ F ☐
3 His chameleon doesn't need a bath. T ☐ F ☐
4 Daniel cleans the tank every day. T ☐ F ☐
5 The chameleon eats insects. T ☐ F ☐
6 The chameleon lives in a tree in the garden. T ☐ F ☐

6 **Think of the story *A new pet* on page 130–131 in your Student's Book. Match the reasons for and against the pets Bob and Alice go to see.**

Pets	Reasons for/against
1 dogs	☐ Alice is afraid of them.
2 cats	☐ They shouldn't be kept in cages.
3 rats	☐ They make too much mess.
4 birds	☐ They're the perfect pet.
5 snakes	☐ They're not great company.
6 goldfish	☐ Alice is really afraid of them.

7 **What do you think these pets are thinking? Write a sentence for each one.**

SB p. 129, 130, 131

A Read the text and answer the questions.

Norman the dog

Norman is a Labrador. He is blind. He lived in a dog sanctuary*. One day Annette came and gave Norman a home. On a sunny day Annette and Norman were on the beach. The beach is the only place where Norman can run freely. Suddenly Norman started running. He heard something. Nobody else could hear it. It was a girl calling for help. Norman jumped into the sea. He found the girl and pulled her back to the beach. A blind dog saved a girl's life.

VOCABULARY: ***sanctuary** – Tierheim

1 What sort of dog is Norman? ....

2 Why is the beach the only place where he can run freely? ....

3 What did Norman hear? ....

4 What did he do? ....

B Read the texts and put the sentences in the correct places.

1 He called for an ambulance.

2 Lulu knew something was wrong.

3 They arrived and solved the problem.

4 But Ringo didn't want to go outside on his own.

RINGO THE CAT

Ray and Carol were in bed. Both of them had headaches and they were very tired. Their cat Ringo wanted to go outside so Carol got up and opened the door. ☐ He looked at Carol. She understood this look and followed him into the garden. Ringo started digging and Carol smelt gas. She called the gas company. ☐ The company told Ray and Carol that the gas leak* was very dangerous. Ringo saved their lives.

Lulu the pig

Sue has an unusual pet called Lulu. Lulu is a pig. One day Sue went away for a few days and her mother JoAnn went to Sue's house to look after Lulu. Suddenly, JoAnn had a heart attack* and fell on the floor. ☐ She ran into the street and sat in the middle of the road to stop the cars. A car stopped. The driver followed the little pig into the house and found JoAnn on the floor. ☐ JoAnn was taken to hospital. The little pig saved her life.

VOCABULARY: ***gas leak** – undichte Stelle in einer Gasleitung; **heart attack** – Herzinfarkt

9 Write a short story about a clever animal. Finish the story with the words ... *saved my life.*

SB p. 132

Essential Grammar *So do/have I. – Neither do/have I.*

10 Match the sentences.

1 I've got a big family.
2 I love horror films.
3 I don't want to go to bed.
4 I haven't got a pet.
5 I don't feel hungry.
6 I've never ridden a horse.
7 I've just finished my homework.
8 I play football for the school team.

☐ So have I. It was really easy.
☐ Neither have I. I'm scared I'll fall off.
☐ So do I. I'm the goalkeeper.
☐ Neither do I. I've just had a big sandwich.
☐ So have I. I've got eight brothers and sisters.
☐ Neither do I. I'm not tired.
☐ So do I. I love getting scared.
☐ Neither have I, but I'd really like one.

11 Complete with *have* or *do*.

1 A I haven't got a mountain bike.
B Neither .... I.

2 A I've already eaten lunch.
B So .... I.

3 A I speak Spanish.
B So .... I.

4 A I don't like chocolate.
B Neither .... I.

5 A I play the piano.
B So .... I.

6 A I haven't seen Bob.
B Neither .... I.

12 Complete with the sentences in the box.

So do I.
So have I.
So have I.
Neither do I.
Neither have I.
Neither have I.

1 A I really like punk music.
B ....

2 A I've got a problem.
B ....

3 A I haven't seen this film yet.
B ....

4 A I've already done my homework.
B ....

5 A I don't want to go to school today.
B ....

6 A I haven't got any money.
B ....

13 Complete the dialogues. Begin with *So* or *Neither*.

1 A I live in Rotterdam.
B So do .... I.

2 A Daniel has got an MP3-player.
B .... I.

3 A I don't know what to do.
B .... I.

4 A I've never been to Paris.
B .... I.

5 A I want to go home.
B .... I.

6 A I've lost my homework.
B .... I.

SB p. 130, 131, 133

6 1 red and feel ill, 2 get it, 3 like you better than me, 4 like films, 5 give her stomach ache, 6 be allergic to them

1 T, 2 F, 3 T
4 Katy a letter, 5 Katy to the cinema, 6 stomach ache
7 Because she might be allergic to flowers. 8 Because Katy's walking towards him. 9 She wants to go to the cinema with William tonight.

8 **A** 1 I only know what I'm not going to do, 2 not going to look after, 3 Is she not going to be, 4 I'm going to phone her then
B Dialogue 1: 1, 5, 3, 2, 6, 4
Dialogue 2: 3, 1, 5, 4, 6, 2

9 1B, 2D, 3A, 4F, 5E, 6C

10 A8, B3, C4, D5, E6, F2, G1, H7

11 1 I'm not going to invite, 2 I'm not going to do, 3 he's not going to tidy / he isn't going to tidy, 4 she's not going to tell / she isn't going to tell, 5 we're not going to have / we aren't going to have

13 6, 4, 2, 3, 1, 5

UNIT 9

1 9 land, 5 spaceship, 4 explode, 13 time machine, 3 universe, 1 galaxy, 11 astronaut, 6 space station, 12 alien, 8 take off, 10 sky, 2 UFO, 7 planet

2 1 time machine, 2 explodes, 3 astronaut, 4 lands, 5 takes off, 6 space station, 7 sky, 8 planets, 9 galaxy, 10 spaceship, 11 aliens, 12 universe, 13 UFO

3 1. Spalte: 6, 3, 1
2. Spalte: 5, 4, 2

4 **A** A2, B5, C6, D3, E1, F4
B **1** 1 Where are you going this time?
2 Yes, there was.
3 Are you going to France, too?
4 You know I love them.
5 They're in the fridge.
2 1 T, 2 F, 3 F, 4 T, 5 F

6 came, found, sat, stopped, started, sent, tried, took, put, barked

7 1 watched, 2 looked, 3 sent, 4 knew, 5 found, 6 started, 7 liked

8 5, 2, 6, 1, 3, 4

9 1 suddenly, 2 At first, 3 The next morning, 4 The next moment, 5 yesterday, 6 Three days later

10 4, 9, 7, 2, 3, 1, 5, 6, 8

12 1 What a pity, 2 That's a shame

14 1 ticket, 2 sold, 3 a shame, 4 pity, 5 showing, 6 expensive, 7 much, 8 please, 9 sit, 10 Row

UNIT 10

1 1 sausage, 2 cabbage, 3 turkey, 4 mineral water, 5 ham, 6 onions, 7 fish, 8 mushroom, 9 plum, 10 strawberry, 11 peach, 12 olive, 13 pear, 14 grapes

2 1 waiter, 2 chef, 3 recipe, 4 waitress, 5 order, 6 menu, 7 bowl

3 Across: 1 potato, 7 pork, 8 strawberry, 9 grapes, 14 pancakes, 15 vegetables
Down: 1 pepper, 2 turkey, 3 onions, 4 cheesecake, 5 pears, 6 cabbage, 10 peaches, 11 rice, 12 lamb, 13 beef

4 1 Rome, 2 Pisa, 3 Milan, 4 Naples

5 **A** 3, 1, 9, 7, 5, 4, 8, 2, 6
B *Possible answers:*
1 Are you ready to order?
2 Would you like peppers maybe?
3 And what would you like to drink?
4 Would you like a dessert?

7 They didn't drink wine. They didn't go with their son. The woman didn't order a pizza. They didn't order spaghetti.

8 3, 2, 5, 4, 6, 1

10 1 T, 2 T, 3 F, 4 T, 5 T, 6 F, 7 F, 8 T, 9 T, 10 T, 11 F, 12 T

11 1 any, 2 some, 3 some, 4 any, 5 some, 6 any

12 6, 5, 4, 1, 3, 2

13 In the fruit bowl …
there are some apples.
there are some grapes.
there aren't any plums.
there are some strawberries.
there aren't any oranges.
there aren't any peaches.

14 1 some, 2 any, 3 any, 4 some, 5 some, 6 some, 7 some, 8 some

15 1 There are some pears.
2 There aren't any strawberries.
3 There are some onions.
4 There are some grapes.
5 There aren't any peppers.
6 There are some tomatoes.
7 There isn't any cabbage.
8 There isn't any lamb.
9 There is some chicken.
10 There is some chocolate.
11 There is some cheesecake.
12 There isn't any cheese.

UNIT 11

1 3 palm, 10 hieroglyphics, 5 papyrus, 6 pharaoh, 13 sacred animal, 4 temple, 12 barefoot, 8 mummy, 9 tomb, 1 pyramid, 2 sphinx, 7 slave, 11 sandals

2 1 leather, 2 horn, 3 ox, 4 wool, 5 sheep, 6 goats

3 1 musician, 2 weaver, 3 juggler, 4 acrobat, 5 scientist, 6 dancer

4 1 temple, 2 religion, 3 pyramid, 4 papyrus, 5 tomb, 6 river, 7 pharaoh, 8 sphinx
The secret word is Egyptian.

5 6 a canary, 1 a servant, 4 a telegram, 7 a candle, 5 treasure, 2 cheek, 8 bandages, 3 a wound

6 3, 6, 7, 1, 8, 2, 9, 5, 10, 4

7 5, 9, 7, 3, 1, 4, 6, 8, 2

8 1 died, 2 put, 3 believed, 4 woke, 5 climbed, 6 knew, 7 guarded, 8 broke, 9 found, 10 stole

9 **A** 1 famous, 2 became, 3 young, 4 died, 5 old, 6 find, 7 found, 8 clothes, 9 mummy
B 1 friend → guide, 2 tourists → scientists, 3 story → curse, 4 shouted → whispered, 5 floor → wall, 6 wind → noise, 7 break → move, 8 window → door, 9 talked → looked

11 man – men, woman – women, child – children, person – people, foot – feet, tooth – teeth, fish – fish, knife – knives, thief – thieves, sheep – sheep

12 1 knives, 2 feet, 3 fish, 4 children, 5 sheep

13 1 children, 2 women, 3 men, 4 teeth, 5 fish, 6 knives

14 A3, B5, C2, D1, E4

15 1 Who phoned you?
2 Who gave Sally a present?
3 Who ate all the chocolate?
4 Who loves Billy?
5 Who lives in that house?
6 Who forgot his homework?
7 Who told you my secret?
8 Who lost her schoolbag?

16 3, 1, 4, 8, 6, 7, 5, 2

UNIT 12

1 1 grandmother, 2 grandfather, 3 uncle, 4 aunt, 5 father, 6 mother, 7 cousin, 8 son, 9 daughter

2 1 single parent, 2 grandparents, 3 twins, 4 cousin, 5 daughter, 6 aunt, 7 children, 8 married, 9 babies

3 1 cousin, 2 married, 3 grandparents, 4 single parent, 5 aunt, 6 twins, 7 babies, 8 children, 9 daughter

4 children, daughter, mother, brother, family, grandparents, uncle, cousin, father, son, aunt, twins, sister

5 1 refugees. 2 Africa. 3 third husband. 4 2006. 5 three children. 6 two children.

6 Mr King: 72, Mrs King: 64, John King: 35, Susan King: 32, The twins: 16, Hanna: 8

7 **A** 1 England, 2 was, 3 raining, 4 go out, 5 played, 6 difficult, 7 easy, 8 juggle, 9 do

8 1 Ron likes playing basketball.
2 Larry likes climbing trees.
3 Maria likes playing football.
4 Cindy likes swimming.
5 Ken likes reading (books).
6 Marina likes playing computer games.

9 1 mustn't, 2 must, 3 must, 4 mustn't, 5 mustn't, 6 mustn't

10 1 Christopher likes dancing, but he doesn't like singing.
2 Harry likes skateboarding, but he doesn't like roller-skating.
3 Ada likes reading, but she doesn't like writing.
4 Tanya likes cooking, but she doesn't like doing the dishes/washing-up.
5 Joe likes juggling, but he doesn't like dancing.
6 My grandpa likes watching TV, but he doesn't like going to the cinema.

12 1 (playing) football, 2 swimming, 3 climbing, 4 getting up, 5 running, 6 riding a/my bike, 7 watching, 8 eating, 9 sleeping

14 1 You must be home by 10 o'clock.
2 10 o'clock as usual.
3 or you'll feel bad all night.
4 Is there anything I can do?

16 1 You mustn't put your shoes on the bed.
2 You mustn't listen to music.
3 You mustn't take food from the fridge.
4 You mustn't run down the stairs.
5 You mustn't use the telephone.

17 5, 1, 3, 7, 9, 11, 4, 10, 6, 2, 8

UNIT 13

1 1 fence, 2 deckchair, 3 doorbell, 4 cooker

2 1 Stacey, 2 Jimmy, 3 Bobby, 4 Poppy, 5 Larry

3 1. Spalte: 1, 9, 7, 11
2. Spalte: 12, 10, 6, 8
3. Spalte: 4, 2, 3, 5

4 1 take, 2 carefully, 3 easily, 4 screaming, 5 done, 6 push, 7 chains, 8 through

1 two hands, 2 right, 3 left
4 second, 5 take their heads off,
6 fighting
7 They mustn't rattle their chains.
8 They walk straight through the walls. 9 He has got the wrong head.

6 1. Zeile: 2, 6, 1
2. Zeile: 4, 5, 3

7 **A** 7, 8, 6, 1, 10, 5, 9, 2, 3, 4
B 1 fence, 2 deckchair, 3 nail, 4 roast potatoes, 5 spells, 6 feather, 7 cooker, 8 sprinkled, 9 car boot, 10 prison

8 1 to Mr Blogg, 2 children / Debbie and Robert, 3 into their ball, 4 put a spell on Mr Blogg, 5 things from Mr Blogg, 6 the brown stuff/liquid on the grass in Mr Blogg's garden / round Mr Blogg's house, 7 a lot of stolen computers in his car boot, 8 Mr Blogg went to prison / Mr Blogg was in prison

10 loud – loudly, quiet – quietly, quick – quickly, slow – slowly, nervous – nervously, careful – carefully, easy – easily, bad – badly, happy – happily, angry – angrily, fast – fast, good – well

11 1 adjective: new, adverb: carefully
2 adjective: dangerous, adverb: nervously
3 adjective: delicious, adverb: quickly
4 adjective: difficult, adverb: badly
5 adjective: naughty, adverb: angrily
6 adjective: old, adverb: fast

12 1 fast, 2 carefully, 3 slowly, 4 happily, 5 badly, 6 well

13 1 well, 2 angrily, 3 quietly, 4 quickly, 5 fast, 6 carefully

14 1 loud, 2 quietly, 3 happily, 4 easily, 5 nervous, 6 quickly, 7 well, 8 angry

UNIT 14

1 5 radiator, 1 sink, 2 cooker, 3 cupboard, 11 bedside table, 6 wardrobe, 8 rug, 4 curtain, 7 television, 10 carpet, 9 armchair

2 1 chair, 2 curtain, 3 carpet, 4 wardrobe, 5 cooker, 6 radiator, 7 fridge, 8 bed
The secret word is cupboard.

3 There are two fridges. There's one chair. There are five beds. There are three tables. There are two radiators. There are two sofas. There's one wardrobe.

4 2, 4, 5, 1, 3

6 **A** **1** 3, 5, 4, 1, 2
2 4, 2, 1, 7, 5, 3, 6

7 1 The homework machine was Professor Albu's idea.
2 The reading machine was Professor Grape's idea.
3 The automatic flower picker was Professor Spalanzani's idea.
4 The pizza machine was Doctor Hoople's idea.
5 The breakfast machine was Doctor Mott's idea.

8 1 Whose idea was the automatic vegetable picker?
2 Whose idea was the automatic vegetable cooker?
3 Whose idea was the automatic vegetable feeder?

9 1 A Whose are those headphones? B They're Monica's.
2 A Whose is that pen? B It's Ben's.
3 A Whose is that backpack? B It's Annabel's.
4 A Whose is that (mobile) phone? B It's Janet's.
5 A Whose is that cap? B It's Nick's.
6 A Whose are those jeans? B They're Sue's.
7 A Whose is that MP3-player? B It's Simon's.
8 A Whose is that guitar? B It's James'.

10 I – my – mine, you – your – yours, he – his – his, she – her – hers, we – our – ours, they – their – theirs

11 1 mine, 2 yours, 3 hers

12 1 ours, 2 mine, 3 his, 4 mine, 5 theirs, 6 Theirs

13 1. Zeile: 3, 6, 2
2. Zeile: 5, 1, 4

14 A What's your bag made of?
B It's made of leather.
A Are you sure?
B Yes, I am. It was really expensive.

C What's your tie like?
D It's blue with white spots. / It's white with blue spots.
C Are you certain?
D No, I'm not. It's white with blue spots. / It's blue with white spots.

UNIT 15

1 1 headache, 2 toe, 3 stomach ache, 4 ankle, 5 oxygen, 6 throat, 7 illness

2 Across: 3 doctor, 4 ear, 6 stomach ache, 9 back, 10 head, 11 knee
Down: 1 toothache, 2 toe, 5 arm, 7 ankle, 8 hand

3 4, 3, 1, 2

4 1 How are you today? – My ankle hurts a bit.
2 Does your leg hurt? – No, it's just my knee.
3 What's the matter? – I've got a pain in my back.
4 Do you feel better today? – No, I've still got a headache.

5 1 Jimmy, 2 Gordon, 3 Michael

7 **A** **1** 20, **2** 2,000, **3** 200,000, **4** 10,000,000, 500
B 1 river, 2 trees, 3 money, 4 farms / fields, 5 plants, 6 medicine, 7 world / planet / earth

8 6, 2, 4, 3, 7, 1, 5

9 go – went – gone, eat – ate – eaten, have – had – had, do – did – done, want – wanted – wanted, play – played – played, see – saw – seen, think – thought – thought, ask – asked – asked, watch – watched – watched, sit – sat – sat, drink – drank – drunk

10 broken, hurt, gone, lost, found, bought, known, fallen, thought, eaten

11 1 have/'ve broken, 2 have/'ve lost, 3 has crashed, 4 have/'ve dropped, 5 have/'ve finished, 6 has had, 7 have/'ve moved, 8 has won

12 1 bought, 2 broken, 3 gone, 4 passed, 5 met, 6 fallen

13 1 Hamilton, 2 dad, 3 Joshua, 4 Patricia, 5 aunt and uncle

14 1 has eaten, 2 have/'ve passed, 3 has gone, 4 have/'ve broken, 5 has fallen, 6 have/'ve, wanted

15 1. Spalte: 2, 1, 4, 3
2. Spalte: 8, 7, 5, 6

UNIT 16

1 1 sunny, 2 thunderstorm, 3 snowy, 4 windy, 5 cloudy, 6 rainy, 7 hot, 8 foggy, 9 cold

2 1 rainy, 2 cold, 3 hot, 4 cloudy, 5 sunny, 6 thunderstorm, 7 foggy, 8 windy, 9 snowy

3 cold, foggy, hot, thunderstorm, rainy, cloudy, sunny, snowy, windy

4 3, 1, 6, 5, 8, 2, 4, 7

5 1 It will be sunny in Madrid.
2 It will be rainy in London.
3 There will be a thunderstorm in Paris.
4 It will be foggy in Turin.
5 It will be snowy in Munich.
6 It will be cloudy in Vienna.

6 1 T, 2 F, 3 F, 4 T, 5 F, 6 T

7 **A** Rain and sun
1 F, 2 T, 3 T, 4 F, 5 F
B The water went away
1 Water from the river started to come into the garden. 2 He went to get some sandbags. 3 The rain stopped and the water went back again. / The water went away.

8 1 help, 2 rain, 3 drive, 4 meet, 5 go, 6 do, 7 tell, 8 finish

9 1 Where's your homework? – I'll bring it tomorrow. I promise.
2 I'm really scared of dogs. – I'm not. I'll get it.
3 Oh! It really hurts. – I'll take you to hospital.
4 I've got lots of homework tonight. – OK, leave it. I'll do it later.
5 This suitcase is heavy. – I'll carry it for you.
6 I haven't got enough money. – I'll give you some.

10 1 I don't think anyone will buy it.
2 I think I'll need my coat today.
3 The test is very easy and you'll pass.
4 You'll sleep really well on this bed.
5 Those berries will make you feel sick.
6 It's made of gold so it will be very expensive.

11 1. Spalte: 2, 3, 1
2. Spalte: 6, 5, 4

12 8, 10, 6, 5, 9, 1, 2, 4, 7, 3

13 *Possible answers:*
1 I'll be rich one day.
2 I'll have a family one day.
3 I'll get/be married one day.
4 I'll be a professor one day.
5 I'll be a sports champion one day.
6 I'll have/ride a horse one day.

UNIT 17

1 12 ice skating, 6 yachtswoman, 16 bike, 3 windsurfing, 14 roller-skating, 1 climbing, 13 trainer, 7 sportsman, 9 score, 11 goalie, 5 yacht, 17 cycling, 15 race, 4 sailing, 2 climber, 10 kick, 8 sportswoman

2 1 tennis, 2 running, 3 snowboarding, 4 football, 5 ice skating

3 1 tennis, 2 volleyball, 3 running, 4 surfing / windsurfing, 5 snowboarding

4 1 favourite, 2 tennis, 3 often, 4 twice, 5 sports, 6 game

5 **A** 4, 1, 7, 2, 5, 3, 6
B 2, 4, 1, 5, 11, 9, 7, 3, 8, 6, 10

6 1 Tommy Caldwell, 2 American, 3 rock climber, 4 He has climbed and speed-climbed walls like The Nose several times. In 2015, he climbed the Dawn Wall. 5 He loves the adventure, the thrill, travelling, seeing the world, pushing himself, and the freedom. 6 to become too obsessed and forget your friends and family, 7 be a good husband and a good dad

7 A3, B5, C1, D2, E6, F4

8 6, 1, 7, 8, 5, 4, 3, 2

9 1 Has he done his homework yet? g) No he hasn't. He's still working it out.
2 Have you seen the new Indiana Jones film yet? b) No, I haven't. Is it on already?
3 Have we arrived yet? e) Another 10 minutes, then we're there.
4 Have you lost your coat? d) Yes, I have. I'm wearing my sister's.
5 Has Harriet's dog had puppies yet? h) Yes, she has. Do you want one?
6 Has she got a new boyfriend yet? f) Yes, she has. His name's Bernie.
7 Have they eaten all of their vegetables? a) No, they haven't so don't give them any ice cream.
8 Has Dad finished cooking dinner yet? c) Yes, he has. We can eat in 10 minutes.

10 1 Have you ever played handball? 2 Have you ever eaten Japanese food? 3 I've never been to the Olympic Games. 4 Have you ever broken your arm? 5 I've never won a competition. 6 My brother has never written a poem.
7 My parents have never been to France. 8 Have you ever cooked dinner for your family?

11 2, 3, 1, 4

UNIT 18

1 2 take your pet to the vet, 7 feed your pet, 4 stroke your pet, 10 brush your pet, 5 give your pet a bath, 1 clean out the litter tray, 6 dry your pet, 3 clean out your pet's cage, 8 play with your pet, 9 walk your pet

2 1 stroking, 2 feeding, 3 cleaning (out), 4 walking, 5 brushing

3 1 Yes, two rats. 2 Yes, their names are Clever and Smart. 3 Yes, that's right. 4 No, they sleep in a box in my room. 5 Yes, they do. Sometimes they come to sleep in my bed. 6 Yes, I do. When I come home from school we play for half an hour.

4 1 Where does it come from? 2 And what colour is it? 3 Is it a difficult pet to keep? 4 How often do you feed it? 5 What does it eat? 6 And where does it live?

5 1 F, 2 T, 3 T, 4 F, 5 T, 6 F

6 3, 4, 1, 6, 2, 5

8 **A** 1 He's a Labrador. 2 Because he is blind. 3 He heard a girl calling for help. 4 He saved the girl's life. / He saved her. He jumped into the sea and pulled her back to the beach.

B 4, 3, 2, 1

10 7, 6, 8, 5, 1, 3, 2, 4

11 1 have, 2 have, 3 do, 4 do, 5 do, 6 have

12 1 So do I. 2 So have I. 3 Neither have I. 4 So have I. 5 Neither do I. 6 Neither have I.

13 1 So do, 2 So have, 3 Neither do, 4 Neither have, 5 So do, 6 So have

14 1 So do I. 2 So do I. 3 So do I. 4 Neither have I. 5 So have I. 6 Neither do I. 7 Neither have I. 8 So have I.

15 1 So do I. 2 So have I. 3 Neither do I. 4 Neither have I. 5 So have I. 6 So do I.